	DATE DUE		

DOÑA MARIA & FRIENDS

Stories from 20 Years
of Missions Work in Colombia

MARION CORLEY

New Hope
Birmingham, Alabama

Published by:
New Hope
P. O. Box 12065
Birmingham, Alabama 35202-2065

Cover design and Illustration by Barry Graham

Bible verses taken from:
King James Version
New American Standard: © Copyright 1960, 1962, 1963, 1968, 1971, 1972, 1973, 1975, 1977 by The Lockman Foundation. A Corporation not for Profit, La Habra, CA. All rights reserved, printed in the United States of America. Used by permission.

Dewey Decimal Classification: B
Subject Headings: MISSIONS—COLOMBIA
             CORLEY, MARION L.
             CORLEY, EVELYN A.
             MISSIONS, FOREIGN
             MISSIONARIES

ISBN: 1-56309-008-2
N924103•5M•0592

Dedication

To Evelyn, my faithful wife.
Without her pulling her part of the load
I would have gone in circles.

To Evelyn's parents, Mr. and Mrs. O. T. Allen,
who provided a stateside home for our children
as each returned to the United States
to continue their education.

To Jesus Christ,
who redeemed us, called us, sent us
and kept His promise,
"Lo, I am with you."

Foreword

These personal reflections of a life of faithful missionary toil will bless and hearten you. The deep sensitivity to the needy hearts of people everywhere, felt so keenly by Marion and Evelyn Corley, shines forth from these pages. Here is a missionary couple who literally poured their lives into the Colombians, to whom they were sent by the Saviour to serve.

Many of the incidents are humorous; you will read them and smile. Occasionally, you will burst into laughter. Some scenes are deeply moving. You will find yourself brushing away a tear or swallowing, with difficulty, a lump in your throat. Every glimpse, without exception, is true to the Word of God, exalts the Saviour, and shows the Father's providential care and direction of His children.

I have had the opportunity of seeing firsthand some of what the Lord used the Corleys to accomplish during their 22 years of service as Southern Baptist missionaries to Colombia. I saw this land of indescribable, expansive beauty. I witnessed the poverty and hurt that defy description. I viewed the country's superstition and spiritual darkness. Amidst these odds, the Corleys served as heralds of God, bearers of the good news, lovers of men for the sake of the gospel.

Only eternity can accurately reveal the number and magnitude of lives changed because Marion and Evelyn were obedient to Him who said, "Go, and I'll go with you." God be praised for their faithfulness. May their tribe increase!

Dr. Gary L. Hearon
Executive Director
Dallas Baptist Association
Dallas, Texas

Introduction

Several years ago, during a World Missions Conference, I shared events about our Baptist work in Colombia. The pastor of the church introduced me by saying, "I know Marion Corley well. We both pastored in Shelby Baptist Association in Alabama before he became a foreign missionary. I also know where he was born: Docena, Alabama. Do you know what verse of Scripture comes to my mind when I think of that? 'Can any good thing come out of Nazareth?' (John 1:46 NASB)."

This pastor knew what he was talking about; he was born in the extreme western side of Birmingham. Docena was three or four miles even farther west. Docena was a small coal mining town. The mining company owned *everything*—the mine, the houses, the school, the commissary (store), and the church (a Baptist preached there one Sunday, a Methodist the next Sunday). The company *almost* owned the people. During the Depression the workers were paid with "clacker," coins that could only be spent at the commissary!

This "Nazareth" didn't have a very good reputation. People from there were known to be tough. Fortunately, both my parents were dedicated Christians, which made up for much of the negative environment. I also had a close relationship with my four brothers and one sister.

My father was a timekeeper at the mine. He trusted in the promises of the Lord. One of his favorite verses was Psalm 37:25, "I have been young, and now am old; yet have I not seen the righteous forsaken, nor his seed begging bread" (KJV).

When I was seven years old, my parents were in a serious automobile accident. Daddy was killed and Mother almost died, too. She never regained her health after the wreck and lived in pain for the rest of her life. We had to move out of the

"Company" house to a small farm. We didn't have much, but "his seed," as Daddy's favorite verse proclaimed, never had to beg bread! We earned it by hard work and through God's goodness.

As I was growing up, I envied some of my friends who had things I didn't have. I wanted three things: to be rich, to be famous, and, then, to serve the Lord. I'm afraid that was my order of priorities. Although I felt the Lord calling me to put Him first, I kept saying, "Lord, I will serve You—but let me do it *my* way!" A dear Christian friend and classmate at Auburn University helped me to see, "Unless He is Lord of *all*, He is not Lord *at* all." On another occasion, a speaker at a Baptist Student Union retreat said, "God's perfect love wants you to have the best. His perfect wisdom knows what is best. Do not be afraid to surrender your life completely to Him." After that, I yielded my will totally to Him. He led me from engineering (where I thought I would find wealth and fame) to music, from music to the pastorate, and from there to foreign missions. He has done more with my life than I could ever have done *my* way!

As you read these personal accounts of our years in Colombia as Southern Baptist missionaries, I think you will agree. There is no room for boasting. It is God who did it and He is due the praise.

Come with me, now, to meet Doña María, her friends, and the many others who touched our lives in Colombia.

Breaking the Ice

We were appointed in 1962 by the Foreign Mission Board of the Southern Baptist Convention to serve as missionaries in Colombia, South America. We had been presented with the needs in several different countries. As we prayed over the choices given us, God impressed on our hearts *Colombia*. Our assignment was to serve as field missionaries—to establish churches in new areas. Our knowledge of the country was very limited, but we had a calm assurance that this was where God wanted us.

Spanish is Colombia's native language, and our knowledge of it was little more than "si, si," and "no, no." We spent our first year in intensive language study in San José, Costa Rica. During that year, the Colombian Baptist Mission (the organization of Southern Baptist missionaries in Colombia) asked us to choose between the cities of Bucaramanga and Neiva. We knew absolutely nothing about either of them. We asked the Lord to help us make the right choice, and after much prayer, we felt a definite leading to Bucaramanga. Many times in the following 22 years we had many confirmations that this was where God wanted us.

The Mission was able to give us some information about Bucaramanga, but we had many unanswered questions. We asked the Lord to put us in contact with someone who could really tell us about "our city."

After finishing language school, we returned to the States to pack our furniture for shipment to Colombia. While there we had several opportunities to share our plans and dreams with churches in the area of Alabama where I had served as pastor before appointment. One day Evelyn, my wife, was speaking to the Woman's Missionary Union organization of one of these churches. After she finished telling them about our intended place of service, one of the women came up to

13

speak to her. She said, "My daughter's college roommate is from Colombia. I think she is from Bucaramanga." Excited, Evelyn asked her, "When could we talk to her? We have a thousand questions to ask her."

A few days later we met the girl, Leonor Olarte. It is hard to say who was the most excited. Leonor was in her first semester at Alabama College in Montevallo (now University of Montevallo), just two miles from where I had pastored. (The next semester she transferred to the University of Alabama, quite a distance away. God's timing was perfect!)

Leonor was thousands of miles from home. As you might expect, she was very homesick. Just the fact that we were going to live in her hometown helped to ease her homesickness. You would have thought we were long lost relatives. We flooded her with questions, and she gave us the answers we needed. She told us, "I am going to write my mother and tell her you are coming. She can help you get to know the city, find a house, find a maid, and help you with shopping. She will be glad to help in any way—except in religious matters, for she is Roman Catholic." When we arrived in 1963, Leonor's mother did all that and more. Ironically, our last 10 years in Colombia we lived only one block from Leonor's mother. We were able to return some of the friendship, especially after she suffered a stroke.

One of our fellow missionaries, Paul Bell, lived in Bogotá, the capital of Colombia. Paul knew a Baptist layman in Bogotá, Lino LaSala Silva. One of Lino's business contacts in Bucaramanga was a man named Gerardo Gutiérrez. Paul and Gerardo were waiting at the airport when we first arrived in Bucaramanga. Gerardo helped us open a bank account. He co-signed our rent contract to guarantee payment and did many other favors for us. He and his family became lifelong friends.

We established our home and began adapting to being "foreigners" in the community. We simply lived among the people, built friendships, and let God manifest His love in and through us. We were the first "gringos" many had ever known.

On one occasion, one of our neighbors asked me why we had come there. I tried to explain that we were there to share with them the love of Christ. "We want to help people develop a personal relationship with God," I said.

She replied, rather abruptly, "We don't need that. We are Roman Catholics!"

Our three children—Bruce, Denise, and Lee Allen—began making friends with other children in the neighborhood. (Bryan and Angela were born later in Colombia.) Little by little, friendly smiles and deeds of kindness began to melt the icy response we felt at first. When a neighbor's wife died in childbirth our expressions of concern laid the foundation for a lasting friendship.

Another time, a neighbor's tomcat helped forge a friendship. We had a female cat, and the tomcat often came to "visit" about midnight. One night, a fierce fight ensued. I was able to separate them and took our neighbor's cat home. Surprisingly, it broke the ice and we became good friends. We learned that one of their sons was a Catholic priest.

Yet another occasion helped the people understand that we cared, although it came at the price of tragedy. One night, we became aware of much excitement in the street. I went outside to see what had happened. A neighbor told me that a small boy had been electrocuted on top of a two story house. I ran up the stairs that opened onto the flat roof of the house. At the front of the house was a wrought iron railing. In front of the railing was a ledge about two feet wide. The boy had been standing behind the railing with a ring of keys in his hand and had dropped them in front of the railing. He had tried to climb over the railing to get them and had slipped and fallen onto the ledge.

The wires bringing electricity to the community ran along this ledge. Someone had peeled off the insulation on the wires, exposing about four inches of each wire, to get "free" electricity during construction. The boy's arm had fallen on these bare wires and he had received 220 volts of electricity.

What a price to pay to save a few pesos!

As you can imagine, people were hysterical. The power company had been called, but we couldn't tell if the power had been turned off. I climbed over the railing and approached the motionless child. Several people began to scream, "Don't touch him! Don't touch him! It will kill you, too!" I assured them I would be very careful. Using a technique I had learned years before as a Boy Scout, I removed my belt, carefully slipped it under his arm and lifted it off the wires. Then I picked him up and handed him across the railing. I climbed back across the railing and gave him artificial respiration but could get no response to my efforts. We carried him downstairs and took him to the nearest clinic, but he was pronounced dead on arrival.

Although we could not save the boy's life, his family and others in the neighborhood began to realize we were there to try to help them.

Where Do We Start?

Our mission in Colombia was to establish Baptist work in Bucaramanga and in the two-state area of Santander and North Santander. That *sounded* simple enough, but where should we start?

Our first week we had Sunday School in our home for our family of five. In the Lord's own timing He sent encouragement the next week. A teenage girl and her mother moved to Bucaramanga from the city of Cali. Neither was a Baptist but the girl had attended a Baptist church in Cali. Don Orr, one of our veteran missionaries, had given her our name and address. With this addition to our group our attendance grew by 40 percent!

The following week we announced we would show a Christian film Sunday night. We invited several of our neighbors, but only three or four came. We projected the picture on our living room wall and put the loudspeaker near the front door, which was left open. As we showed the film, several people walked up to our house and began watching from the doorway. Others stood in our flowerbed looking through the window.

The next time we presented a film, we did it differently. We hung a bed sheet over the front window and projected the image onto it. The loudspeaker was placed *in* the doorway so people inside and outside could hear. This time several more people came inside. A large crowd gathered in our front yard and in the street. They saw the picture in reverse, but that didn't seem to matter to them.

Little by little, new people began coming to our Bible studies. Eventually, we needed more seating. Colombia did not have a church furniture company, so I designed and built a comfortable slat bench and simple pulpit.

As the group outgrew our living room and dining room, we

began looking for a house to rent to serve as a temporary location for the mission. We found one a block from our home which would meet our needs. The owner was willing to rent it to us for a reasonable price. However, on the day we were to meet at the rental agency to sign the contract, he didn't show up. We later learned, through a mutual friend, that the Catholic priest in the community had told him he should not rent it to us. We began the search again and found another. This one was two and a half blocks from our house. Our friend Gerardo co-signed this contract, also. Not many people would go "out on a limb" for a newcomer, but that action showed how much of a friend he had become.

The house we rented for the mission, like many houses in Colombia, had the garage *in* the house. The garage door and entrance door were side by side; no wall separated them. Not only that, an open stairway that led to the second floor was all that separated the garage from the living room. The living room opened into the dining room, with no wall between them. This layout gave us lots of open space.

I hired a carpenter to build five more benches patterned after the one I had made. These six benches and the pulpit were placed in the garage area, which became our worship center. We bought folding chairs for the living and dining area to give us flexibility and room for growth. During Sunday School Evelyn taught the children upstairs. I taught the young people and adults in the worship center. It was here that we first came to know Doña María.

As long as the services were held in our home, we used our own piano, which Evelyn played reasonably well, to accompany the singing. In the new location we had no piano. We did have a second-hand accordion which Evelyn could play some, but she had never quite mastered it.

One day, I asked her, "If the chord buttons and keyboard were side by side, could you play it?" She thought she could, so I began to fashion in my mind how this could be done. I made a cabinet similar to a pump organ with an air-tight chamber. I

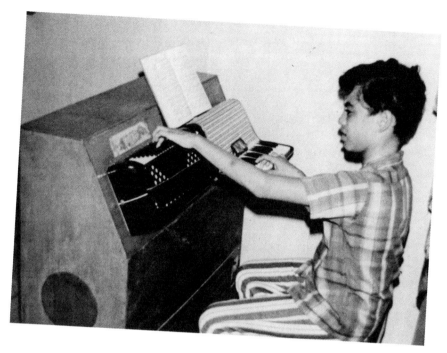

An example of Marion Corley's inventiveness, this organ was built from a second-hand accordion. The organ served for many years in worship services in Bucaramanga and, later, at other mission points.

took the bellows (the middle, flexible part) out of the accordion and mounted the chord buttons to the left of it and the keyboard to the right. Then I mounted an old vacuum cleaner motor to the cabinet so it would blow air into the chamber. This delivered a large volume of air, but it didn't have enough pressure to make the reeds vibrate sufficiently to create sound. I replaced the vacuum cleaner motor with a rebuilt refrigerator compressor. Our oldest son, Bruce, helped me with the project, but he had some doubts it would work. When the compressor was in place, we took a deep breath and plugged it in. It worked! This experience gave birth to a family expression we still use, "There is only one thing wrong with it—it works!"

The chord organ served our needs in the worship services until a North American family, who worked for an oil company, came to live in Bucaramanga. They brought a piano for the church along with their own furniture. The chord organ also served us when we started a church in another city, some years later. When it was no longer needed as an organ, I took it apart and put the bellows back in it to serve again as an accordion. This was used in various new mission points started by that second church.

The methods we used to reach people for Christ were many and varied: preaching, teaching, visiting in homes, and training leaders. From these experiences we learned to express ourselves, not only in a foreign language, but also in terms the people clearly understood. For example, "baptism" in a Catholic country is usually understood as christening an infant. "Praying" means saying the rosary.

In dealing with such hindrances, we learned that living a Christ-centered life was the most effective method of witnessing. Christ's love manifested in daily contact was clearly understood.

We were constantly faced with new challenges, but the Lord helped us develop talents we didn't know existed, both in ourselves and in the people we worked with.

What Did You Say?

Our first year after appointment as missionaries was spent in San José, Costa Rica, in language school. It was a humbling experience to be taught, as if we were children, a new language. It was *very* important to learn to speak the language of the people we would work with. We didn't learn English in a year, so it was unreasonable to expect to learn a foreign language in such a short time. That year of intensive study, however, gave us a foundation for a lifetime of learning. Our major assignment our second year as missionaries (our first year in Colombia) was to continue our study of Spanish, using a private tutor. When your purpose is to communicate the message of eternal life, you need to learn to say what you mean. At the same time, there are some very amusing things that happen when you *don't* say what you mean.

While we lived in San José, we enjoyed the beauty of exotic, tropical flowers throughout the year. One woman came by our house once or twice a week selling freshly cut flowers. The flowers were very inexpensive and we usually bought some. One day as I left the house I met her about a half a block away. She asked me, "Do you want to buy flowers today?"

"My wife is at home," I answered. "Ask her if she wants some."

The woman knocked at our door, and when Evelyn answered, she said, "Your husband sent me with these flowers."

Evelyn said, "They are beautiful," and took them from her. Then she added (she thought), "Did my husband pay you?"

"What?"

"Did my husband pay you?"

"I don't understand!"

Fortunately, our maid was nearby and entered the conversation. She asked the woman how much the flowers cost, and then Evelyn paid her. As Evelyn and the maid closed the door, the maid said, "Do you know what you asked her?" Then motioning with her fist to her chin, she said, "The word is *pagar* (to pay) not *pegar* (to hit)!"

Humorous mistakes are not confined to students at language school. Once one of the single missionaries in Colombia planned to visit an isolated country church with two national pastors. The only way to get there was by mule. The pastors were leading the way. The reins of her mule's bridle were made of rope and along the way they slipped out of her hands. She couldn't reach them, so she called out to the pastors, "Me cayó la ropa!" She *thought* she was saying, "My rope fell." The pastors stopped but they did not seem to know what to do. She repeated her statement. Still they were puzzled as to what they should do. Finally one ventured to look back, then went to her aid. He explained to her that *ropa* does not mean rope, it means clothes!

Another veteran missionary was preaching about Jesus healing a paralytic. He intended to quote Jesus' command, "Arise, and take thy bed, and walk" (Mark 2:9 KJV). When he did, the congregation began to chuckle. Puzzled, he continued his sermon. A little later he repeated the same expression. More laughter ensued—and more puzzlement on his part. When the sermon ended someone helped him understand his mistake. The verb *tomar* can mean "to take up" or "to drink," depending on the noun it is used with. He had used the wrong noun. Instead of saying "Arise, take up thy bed (*lecho*) and walk!" he had said, "Arise, drink your milk (*leche*)!" No wonder the people had chuckled!

On still another occasion, a missionary was preaching at the Colombian Woman's Missionary Union Annual Convention. His message focused on the expression, "Man looks on the outside but God looks on the heart." Each point of his sermon repeated this expression. Each time he said it, a ripple of laughter ran through the audience. When the message was over, he couldn't wait to ask, "What caused the laughter?"

Can you imagine his chagrin when he found out he had actually said, "God is looking at your underwear!"

I made more than my share of mistakes, also. As we were approaching the end of our first term of service, I told our congregation they needed to be faithful in their giving, so they could support their new pastor. The verb *soportar* sounded correct to me. However, a church member suggested I needed to use a different word. What I had actually said was, "You need to tolerate your pastor!"

When we returned to the field after furlough, my family stayed in Bogotá while I went to Bucaramanga to locate a house to rent. I stayed in a hotel and the next morning went to the restaurant to eat breakfast. I *thought* I ordered orange juice, coffee, toast, and oatmeal. First, the waiter brought the juice, hand squeezed, from tree-ripened oranges. Delicious! Next, he brought the toast, with tropical fruit jelly and coffee. This I enjoyed, also. Would the oatmeal come later? Why was it taking so long to cook? After a while the waiter brought me the check. I sat there reflecting on what I had said when I placed my order. My mistake finally dawned on me. I had chosen the wrong word, and the waiter was too kind to tell me my mistake, nor did he want to serve me what I had ordered. The word I should have said was *avena*. I had said *arena*. He kindly did not bring the bowl of *sand* I had ordered!

In spite of our errors, the Colombians seemed to understand what we were there to say. The heart of the gospel is love. The Scriptures say, "If I speak with the tongues of men and of angels, but do not have love . . ." (1 Cor. 13:1 NASB). Love is expressed not as much with the mouth as with the heart and life.

I Want to Be a Christian

Sunday by Sunday we could see a gradual increase in the attendance at our mission. We had Sunday School in the morning and the worship service at night. About once a month we showed a Christian film. For all these services we would leave both the main entrance door and the garage door open. Passersby usually stood on the sidewalk listening, especially when we showed a film. Some would listen briefly and continue on their way. Others would come inside.

One morning as we were singing, an obviously poor, short, fat, old woman stopped to listen. Someone in the group invited her in. At first she said no, but after a second invitation she hesitantly came in and sat on the end of one of the benches, close to the door.

She seemed to be soaking up every word spoken. When I teach a group I always try to get the people to participate through asking them questions and encouraging their comments. Since this woman was so attentive, I asked her a simple question related to the lesson. She looked up at me and said, "Señor, I'm old and forgetful. I'm sorry, but I can't answer your question."

I thought to myself, "Marion, you have blown it now! She will never come back." But she did. She came every Sunday. Her name was Doña María.

The words "short, fat, old, and poor" described Doña María well. (Throughout this book, you will encounter the terms *Doña* and *Don* used with names of persons. Each is a title of respect. Don is used with a man's first name, Doña with a woman's. In everyday society the terms are used to refer to people of prominence and/or wealth. Among Christians they are used freely, regardless of rank.) She was less than 5 feet tall, and she weighed almost 200 pounds. She was about 65-years-old, but the deep lines in her face made her look older.

On her second visit I asked her where she lived, so I could visit her. She did not give an address, but instead simple instructions on how to get to her home. It was about six blocks from the mission, on the right-of-way of a street that had been started but never finished. The money had run out and construction had been abandoned.

The term that best describes her home is "squatter's shack." The front door was made of three rough planks nailed together. When I dropped by to visit, it was partially open. I called out, "Doña María, are you home?"

"Yes, come in," she answered, from inside. There were no windows, so the only light came through the door and the cracks in the walls. I ducked my head and entered, for I was taller than the roof.

Doña María motioned for me to sit down on a small wooden box, the best seat in the house. Her house consisted of only one small room, about nine feet square in size. The frame was made of round poles cut from small trees. The roof was almost flat and was made of second-hand tin that leaked when it rained. One wall consisted of oil drums that had been split open and flattened. The other walls were made of rough lumber, cardboard, and "tar paper." Doña María cooked on a one-burner kerosene stove that sat on a wooden box. Her combination kitchen sink, wash basin, and bath tub was an aluminum pan. There was no running water; she carried it from about a block away. There was also no electricity.

Three rough boards laying on bricks served as a bed. The boards were covered with paper cement sacks that had been torn open and spread out. She had no mattress of any kind.

In talking to her I learned that she had no regular source of income. She earned a little money washing and ironing clothes in people's homes.

During the next 15 years, Doña María lived with us part of the time. She became like one of our family. Our two youngest children, Bryan and Angela, almost thought of her as their grandmother. During those years, she told us about her childhood, marriage, children, and the many hardships she had faced.

If you ask most people in Colombia if they are Christians, they will answer yes. They may add, "My parents had me baptized when I was an infant." They have been taught that this action makes them Christians. Any child who has not been baptized is considered an animal. Because of this concept, when persons make a personal profession of accepting Christ as Saviour, the Colombian Baptist churches do not immediately baptize them. First they are given training in the basic concepts of what it means to be a Christian. As our group gradually developed, five participants made professions of faith and desired to be baptized. We had tried to teach them not only what it meant to accept Christ, but also the responsibility of following Him.

The Emmanuel Baptist Church of Bogotá sponsored us as a mission, and they sent their pastor to help us evaluate and counsel these new believers. We wanted to make sure they understood that they could face rejection by friends and family. During the Sunday School time one morning, we announced, "All those who want to be baptized, please meet with us at three o'clock this afternoon."

When the appointed hour arrived, the five we had expected came, as did Doña María. I remember thinking, "Poor soul, she doesn't even know what this meeting is all about." We began asking the others, one by one, to share briefly their personal experience and what it meant to them to be a true Christian. I didn't ask Doña María the questions because she had not made an open profession of faith like the others had.

We finished talking to the candidates and told them we felt they were mature enough to be baptized. We closed with prayer and started to leave. Doña María came to me and said in a very mild voice, "Pastor, I'm an old woman and I can't remember things, but I want to be a Christian. I want to be baptized."

As you can imagine, it took only a moment to get the

The first group to be baptized in Bucaramanga. Doña María (third from right) earnestly requested: "Pastor, I'm an old woman and I can't remember things, but I want to be a Christian. I want to be baptized." The author, Marion Corley, is at far right.

committee together again. We asked Doña María to share with us what she understood being a Christian meant. Her answers were simple, but they showed us she was truly placing her faith in Christ as her Saviour. She, too, was approved by the committee.

We had no baptistry, so we asked another evangelical church if we could use theirs. They were happy to do so. The next Sunday afternoon we shared the thrill as these six experienced the public declaration of their newfound faith. Through the years that followed, Doña María was one of the most faithful of those to whom we ministered. She was a source of inspiration and blessing to us in many ways.

Mister, Can You Read?

Doña María's capacity to learn was not as rapid as some of the other new Christians. She attended only one day of school in her lifetime. She told us that she grew up in a very remote part of the country. When she was old enough to go to school, her mother sent her with some other children to a little one-room school. Her father did not know about it beforehand, however. When she came home from school that first day, he said to her, "Don't go back to that school. I need you to help me farm."

Her father's attitude toward her working was evident in several ways. Her skin was deeply bronzed and wrinkled from years of outdoor labor in the tropical sun. One of her fingers was missing, also. When I asked her how she lost it, she told me that when she was very young her father assigned her the task of feeding the sugar cane into the cane mill. She and a sister were playing as they worked. Before she knew it, her hand was caught in the mill. "Fortunately, the mill was powered by a lazy mule which was stopped before I got my whole hand mashed off," she chuckled.

Doña María couldn't read or write; an X was her signature. She wanted so much to learn to read the Bible, however. During one spell when she lived with us, our 10-year-old daughter, Angela, would go into Doña María's room at night and read the Bible to her. Angela taught Doña María a few letters of the alphabet. When Doña María learned to recognize "Jesus," both were thrilled!

Doña María was old and sometimes forgetful, by her own admission. Her eyesight, also, was growing dim. Yet it was thrilling to see her grow spiritually as she learned that God loved her so very much. After all, being a child of the King made her a princess! She wanted to help others learn what she knew, so that they might find the same joy. Among her friends it was easy to tell them what the Lord was doing in her life, but she wanted to tell others, also. How could an old, illiterate do that? Doña María soon discovered her own style.

One Sunday I used a sermon illustration that gave her an idea. When she left the church, she took a tract from the rack by the door and started home. As she walked toward her shack, she prayed she would encounter someone to share with. She saw a man who was building his house. He was a complete stranger, yet she approached him and said, "Mister, can you read?"

He answered, "Why, sure!"

She said, "I got this paper at church, but I can't read. Would you read it to me?"

He laid down his hammer, took the tract, and began to read it aloud. It told how all men are sinners and that God can't let people with sin in their lives into heaven. Doña María said, "That's bad news, isn't it?" He continued to read how God loves us, although we are sinners. Doña María commented, "I'm glad to hear that!" The man continued reading about how Christ came to earth to die in our place for our sins. "That's good news, isn't it?" she said. Then the tract explained that if we confess our sins to God, He will forgive us, give us eternal life, and allow us to live with Him in heaven. Doña María said, "That's the best news I ever heard!"

The man folded the tract and started to hand it back to Doña María. She said, "Why don't you keep it, since I can't read?" We never learned the man's name. However, when I get to heaven, I will not be surprised if I meet him, as well as many others who will say, "Doña María showed me the way!" Nor will I be surprised to see that her heavenly home does not look at all like her earthly shack. Jesus said, "I go to prepare a place for you" (John 14:2*b* NASB). Hers will be a mansion, I have no doubt!

Deceived But Not Destroyed

As time passed, Doña María told us more about her life. Some of the events she told were humorous, while others were heartwrenching.

When Doña María was a child, her family lived far in the country. The closest town was a small one several miles away. No regular transportation existed, so when her family went to town they usually walked. As you can imagine, they didn't go very often. The town was so small it didn't even have a Catholic church. In such cases a priest was assigned to the area. Once a month he visited to hear confessions and celebrate mass.

Doña María's family was not very religious, but they went to this "church" occasionally to confess and to attend mass. The altar was portable, set up under the shade of a big tree. The confessional consisted of a chair in which the priest sat and a small pad on which the person who was confessing knelt at the priest's feet.

When Doña María was 11 or 12, her family went to this town when the priest was scheduled to be there. Her parents left her with several others waiting to confess while they went to a store to buy supplies. The other people in line finished and left. Young María was last. María knelt before the priest and began to confess her sins. The priest put his hand on her shoulder, then moved it toward her chest. Slowly he reached inside her dress and began fondling her breast! Young María panicked! She jumped to her feet and ran to find her parents. She was afraid to tell them what had happened, however, as she knew the priest would deny it. If her father believed her he would likely attack the priest. He might even kill him! She decided to keep the incident to herself.

As you can imagine, this event adversely affected Doña María's faith. She determined in her heart never again to trust priests nor attend the Catholic church. It almost destroyed her faith in God.

As the years rolled by, she still felt a hunger in her soul to know God. Occasionally, she attended a Protestant church with friends who seemed sincere and appeared different because of their faith. She needed to know that God loved her, but she still had many doubts and questions. Could He really love someone as poor as she was? She had done many things she knew God did not like. Could she really be forgiven and find peace? Where could she find the truth? Years later, at age 65, when she wandered into our mission, she began the spiritual journey that transformed her life through the power and grace of God.

Go Get My Tobaccos!

Doña María's life was not what you would consider ordinary. She and her mother had been bought by the man for whom they worked; he branded them on the hip to show they belonged to him. Slavery was not officially recognized then in Colombia, but it was still practiced in remote areas.

When Doña María was 14-years-old, a friend of her father's asked him if he could marry her. Her father agreed, and Doña María and the man were married. This freed her from her "master," only to make her a slave of another sort. She still worked as hard as before, but now had additional obligations as a wife. She bore a total of 13 children, with only a midwife in attendance. Several of them died at birth or shortly after.

Somewhere along the way, Doña María began to smoke cigars, called "tobaccos" among the country folk. Her husband went to town on weekends to get drunk with his friends, and he usually returned well into the night. It did no good for her to complain about these trips. The only thing she demanded of him was that he bring her a supply of tobaccos.

One weekend he left as usual for a night of drinking. When he returned, she asked, "Did you bring my tobaccos?"

He replied, "No, I forgot them."

"Just turn around and go back and get them," she answered.

"I'll get them tomorrow."

"Go get my tobaccos. I need them now!" she exclaimed.

He did as she said, knowing how severe her addiction was.

For many years Doña María knew that her smoking was bad for her health. She also felt it was a filthy habit and a waste of money. Over 40 years she had tried a number of times to quit, but had not been able to do so.

When she gave her heart to the Lord, she asked Him to take away her craving for tobacco. The Lord answered that prayer! Later, when she talked to her unsaved friends about the Lord, she shared her victory with them. She proudly proclaimed, "If the Lord did that for me, just think what He can do for you!"

Thief, Come Back!

At one time Doña María lived with her son in a squatter's shack on the right-of-way of a country road. The shack was built of bamboo and palm leaves, and, as you can imagine, it was not very secure. Doña María didn't have many worldly belongings, but her most prized possession was a small transistor radio. One day she returned to her home to discover the radio was gone. She never told us why, but she had a strong feeling the man in the shanty next door had taken it.

The next day Doña María saw the man rolling a wheelbarrow down the road. She called out to him and invited him in for a cup of coffee. Once inside, she began to tell him about the theft. She said, "That radio was one of the few things I owned. I enjoyed listening to music and preaching on it. If whoever took it knew how much I miss it, they couldn't enjoy listening to it. They would probably bring it back."

The two finished their coffee and the man left. A few minutes later he returned and handed Doña María the radio. He said, "Here is your radio. Please forgive me for taking it. I didn't know it meant so much to you!"

The Ministry of Prayer

Doña María had a real ministry in our lives. One example of it was her prayer support.

One day I met a man who had moved to Bucaramanga from Bogotá, the capital city of Colombia. He shared with me a difficult situation. He had worked for the government, but, as is so often the case with a change of government, he had lost his job. A new administration often replaced employees with people of their political persuasion.

Another event added to his crisis. His home had been robbed, resulting in the loss of his television and several other valuable items. His car had been stolen, also. Cars are very expensive in Colombia, and owners cannot insure them for theft except for a fraction of their value. This series of events had been especially hard on the man's wife. She was so depressed that she was on the verge of suicide.

Our church promised to pray for the man and his family. We would especially pray that he would be able to find work. For several weeks he attended church each Sunday and brought several of his children.

One morning he called me at home. "Pastor," he said, "you remember that I told you about my wife's depression? Yesterday she took a large dose of rat poison. When we discovered this, we rushed her to the hospital, but during the night she died."

I asked him where he was, and he said, "At the church." I asked him to wait there for me and I left immediately.

As expected, he shared with me his grief as a heartbroken, confused man. He said, "Why would God let all this happen to us?" I responded as best I could and expressed my deep concern. He said, "I don't know what I am going to do. As you know, I have been without work. My wife's family in Medellín is wealthy, but they have always looked down on me. I can't call on them for help." I told him that we would be glad to help him in every way possible.

One of the young men of the church happened to be present working. I asked him to call some of the funeral homes and ask the price of a modest funeral. Also present was a woman who served as caretaker of the church. (Even the churches needed someone, day and night, to guard against thieves!) The young man and the caretaker joined us as we prayed for God's direction and comfort.

The man asked, "Can you give me the address of the Sunday School superintendent, Victoriano Stephens? I want to ask him if he and his wife can keep my children during this time when everything is so uncertain."

I told him I did not have Victoriano's exact address with me, but I would be glad to take him there. On our way, he expressed more questions and confusion. He said that the police had requested that he return to the hospital by 10:00 A.M. They wanted to question him, along with the doctor who was performing an autopsy. He asked, "Why do they want an autopsy? Why can't I just bury her?" I told him it was routine procedure in a death like this, and added it was good that it would be cleared up now, so there would be no question later about the cause of her death. Since his wife's family had not accepted him, they might possibly raise questions later. Then it would become necessary to exhume her body in order to determine the cause of death, and that would only add to his grief.

When we arrived at Victoriano's home, no one was there, so we started for the hospital. I suggested that we stop back by my home to get something to drink. Though I did not tell my friend, my reason for stopping by home was to get some cash in case the funeral home required a partial payment in advance.

When we arrived home, another young man from the church was waiting to talk with me. I asked Doña María to fix a soft drink for each of us. As we talked, the grief-stricken man expressed a desire to let a certain pastor in Bogotá know what had happened. This pastor had baptized him, his wife, and two of their children. I checked our directory of churches but discovered no telephone listing for this church or the pastor. I told him I would call one of our missionaries, Tommy Norman, so he could get word to the pastor.

Tommy's wife, Joan, answered my call. I explained the situation to her, and she said they would pass the news to the pastor and the church.

When we arrived at the hospital, we went to the fifth floor and asked a nurse at the desk if Dr. Rojas had arrived. She said no. While we waited the man asked more questions, such as, "What am I going to do with the children? Why would my wife want to do a thing like this? What will her family say?"

After waiting quite a while, he said, "I wonder what is taking so long? Did I misunderstand the doctor? He mentioned something about the seventh floor." I said perhaps they were not finished with the autopsy, and suggested that I go to the morgue on the first floor while he checked to see if Dr. Rojas was on the seventh floor. We agreed to meet back on the fifth floor.

When I arrived at the morgue, I asked if they had finished the autopsy. The person in charge looked at me with a puzzled expression and said, "No, we haven't done an autopsy on anyone this morning." I went to the emergency desk and asked if the man's wife had been admitted during the night. The clerk checked her records carefully and said no. I then returned to the fifth floor and asked the nurse at the desk if the man had returned. Not surprisingly, she said no.

I asked, "Has Dr. Rojas been by?"

"No, we don't have a Dr. Rojas working on this floor."

Just to cover all bases, I went to the seventh floor. I was not too surprised when the person in charge said she had not seen the man I described, nor did she know a Dr. Rojas! I headed home.

As you can imagine, many questions filled my mind now.

This was not the first time someone had tried to pull a fast one on me. But the one thing that kept coming back to my mind was he had never asked me for even one peso! How could anyone expect to get money for a funeral without a body? He certainly had an elaborate scheme. At least he did not get any money from us!

When I returned home, Doña María met me at the front door, relieved. She said, "Don Mario, I'm so glad to see you are all right. I've been praying that God would take care of you. That man is no good!"

Neither the caretaker at the church, the man who was working there, nor the young man who was waiting at my house doubted the man's story. Yet this woman in her late seventies and with no education had heard only a part of my conversation on the phone and had seen through him when none of the rest of us had.

Doña María was uneducated, but she wasn't dumb!

Get the Gringo!

The term *gringo* is a familiar word in Spanish-speaking countries. In Colombia it usually means someone from the United States; the context and tone of voice reveals the full meaning. Friends often use it as a term of admiration. They admire the way Americans do things. Others, especially if they are of Communist orientation, use it as a strong, negative insult. This story was definitely of the latter case!

After we had been in Colombia about two-and-a-half years, the Mission asked me to direct construction of the Betania Baptist Church in Bogotá. I had some experience in construction prior to appointment by the Foreign Mission Board. Mission policy was to ask more seasoned missionaries to do this sort of thing, but the need was urgent. Missionary Wilson Donehoo had begun the project and carried it through the planning stage. (Another missionary lived in Bogotá, but he had no construction experience.) The actual construction had already begun—the foundations were poured and some of the concrete columns had been constructed.

Wilson was scheduled to return to the States for furlough in about two months. He was director of the Baptist Book Store, which was a full-time job, and he had other responsibilities as well.

At the time, our work in Bucaramanga was centered around weekend activities. Every other week I would fly to Bogotá on Monday and return to Bucaramanga on Friday or Saturday, depending on the problems that needed to be worked out with the contractor. Sometimes I had to go every week.

While the Donehoos were still in Bogotá, I stayed in their home. They lived about three blocks from the main entrance to the National University, which was a hotbed of Communist activities. Students held frequent strikes and demonstrations, burned cars or buses, and clashed with the police. Rock throwing and tear gas counterattacks were not rare!

One afternoon about dusk, I was returning from the construction site to the Donehoo's. About three blocks from the university entrance, students had partially blocked the street. A young man held up his hand, indicating for me to stop. As he approached the car, I rolled down the window. He said, "Sir, this street is closed."

"I would like to go just one more block, turn right, and go two blocks to reach my destination."

"If you attempt that, you will run into serious trouble. I would advise you to turn around and go some other route," he answered. I didn't want trouble, so I began to turn around.

At that moment another student several feet away looked my way. He recognized that I was a foreigner and started toward the car. He had half a brick in one hand and a large rock in the other. He called out, "A gringo! Let's get him!" He drew back his arm to throw the brick through the windshield. He probably would *not* have stopped with that! The young man standing beside the car called out, "Stop! Leave him alone. He is cooperating with us and is leaving."

I turned the car around and tried to find a different route. "Thank You, Lord, for the kindness of the first young man!" I prayed.

There was no other route open which would take me to the Donehoo's home. I had to take an around-about way to get even close. A deep drainage ditch ran between this section and the house. However, it had only a foot bridge across it. I could find no place to cross over in the car. It is never safe to leave a car on the streets of Bogotá, but especially so during a riot. As I drove down the street approaching the foot bridge, I looked for a house with an empty garage. I spotted an unoccupied one with a grill-type door. I knocked on the door of the home. When the woman of the house, a total stranger, opened the door, I explained the situation to her and asked if I could put the car in her garage until things calmed down. To my surprise she said, "Certainly. I will be most happy to help you." From there I walked to the Donehoo's home. "Thank You, Lord, for leading me there," I again prayed.

Fortunately, things cooled down after dark. I walked back to the house, thanked the woman profusely, and drove back around to the Donehoo's.

In many areas of the world, people love the United States and dream of living here some day. Others hate America just as strongly. It would be nice if we could go in the name of Jesus to share God's love and everyone received us with open arms and loved us in return. It just does not happen that way, however. Even Jesus, God's Son, was hated by those who should have loved Him. He told us, "And you will be hated by all on account of My name, but it is the one who has endured to the end who will be saved" (Matt. 10:22 NASB). He also said, "Blessed are you when men hate you . . ." (Luke 6:22a NASB).

Protecting a Fool

We learned many things from our Colombian friends over the years. Some things we first considered superstitious or foolish. Afterwards, we discovered *we* were probably the foolish ones!

For example, a woman who ironed for us taught us something that we first thought was foolish. One day our daughter Angela fell and hit her head on the corner of a concrete step. A knot the size of an egg rose on her forehead immediately. The woman ran into the kitchen and cut a potato in half. She brought one piece to Evelyn and said, "Hold this on the bump until I get back." She returned to the kitchen, scraped the other half into a paste and plastered it on the ugly bruise. "Keep this there as long as you can," she instructed. After about an hour she took it off. The bump had gone down; the next day you could not even tell that Angela had bumped her head! This woman had practically no education, yet she knew many things we didn't.

Most all Colombian homes had an aloe plant hanging in a corner of the house. It is the first thing Colombians reach for when they are burned. They learned about its curative powers centuries before the "gringos" did!

My most memorable experience in this regard occurred after we had been in Colombia about three years. To this day, when I think of it I am both frightened and thankful.

One Saturday I decided to take the children out in the country for a walk. As we walked along a little stream, nine-year-old Lee Allen said, "Daddy, look at that pretty little frog. Catch him for me and I will take him to science class." I reached down and picked it up. I held it in my hand for 30 minutes or more. At one point I put it in my shirt pocket for a few minutes while I tied a shoelace. When I helped move a large rock I handed it to Lee Allen for a few minutes.

When it was time to go home, we climbed back up the hill

to where I had parked the car. I looked for something in which we could put the frog. The only thing available was an empty soft drink bottle. The frog was so small it went in the mouth of the bottle with room to spare.

On Monday Lee Allen carried the frog to school. When he came home at lunch, he said, "Daddy, my teacher said that frog is poison." I chuckled and said, "That's just another of their strange ideas. When I was a kid we played with frogs all the time. People said they would cause warts on you, but I don't think they even do that."

I forgot all about the frog. A few weeks later the May 1966 issue of *National Geographic* arrived in the mail. The main article that month was, "Capturing Strange Creatures in Colombia." I began to read the article. It told about a scientist who traveled to Colombia to find a certain type of frog for medical research. Colombian Indians use them to poison darts for hunting. The frogs don't bite, the article said, but they secrete a deadly poison from the pores of their skin. *It is the most potent venom known!* From one tiny frog comes enough poison for 50 darts, and it causes death in a matter of minutes!

I recalled what the frog we had captured looked like. I was certain it was identical to the one discussed in the article. If there had been even the slightest break in the skin on my hands, I would not have lived to be writing this. Lee Allen could have suffered the same fate. As I read the article, chills ran down my spine. I prayed, "Thank you, Lord, for protecting a fool!"

The Short Cut

During our years of missionary service in Colombia, I drove many miles over winding mountain roads. The scenes were breathtaking—high mountains and deep gorges with sheer drops of 1,000 feet or more, right at the edge of the road (and usually no guard rail!). I had constant opportunities for a private audience with the Lord, thanking Him for the beauty of His creation or for His protective hand in times of danger.

Frequently, when I arrived at my destination, someone would ask me, "Did you come alone?" My answer was always, "No, the Lord came with me!" I never felt alone, for the same One who said, "Go . . . ," also said, "Lo, I am with you always. . . ."

On one memorable trip my family and a Colombian friend traveled with me. We were going to the city of Sogamoso to assist the church for several days. On the map I noticed a road across the mountain which would be much shorter than going through Tunja, on the main road. It looked like it might save an hour or more. I asked our Colombian friend, "Carlos, have you traveled that road before?" He answered, "Yes, buses go that way all the time." I should have questioned him further, but in my haste I didn't. We turned off at the small town of San Gil and headed over the mountains towards the town of Duitama. The road was unpaved but acceptable at first. However, the higher we climbed into the mountains, the worse the road became.

We were traveling in a small, low-slung car not made to fit the ruts the buses had made. The ruts became deeper as we progressed. Frequently the car would drag on a high spot, but at least we were making progress. Then it began to rain. Suddenly, we hit a deep rut. We heard a loud *thud* and the sound of scraping metal. My first thought was, "Well, I have pulled the muffler off. Since the car is running poorly, and we might meet a bus coming down the mountain, I think I'll just leave the muffler in the road." Fortunately, I had second thoughts and stopped to check it out. When I looked under the car, I discovered the gas tank, not the muffler, had been torn loose! If we had tried to continue, we would have risked catching the car on fire. I crawled under the car to see if I could fix it. The front of the tank was on the ground. The back side was still suspended by a rusty bracket, but the copper fuel line had ruptured and gas was pouring out, making a puddle. I put my finger over the hole. I sure didn't want to get caught on that mountain without gas!

I called out to my family and Carlos to let them know what had happened. I saw no need to add to their alarm by reminding them that one of Colombia's most notorious bandits had been operating in that area in recent weeks. Our oldest son, Bruce, about 14 at the time, got out of the car. He walked to the side of the road and looked over the valley below. After a few moments he came back to the car and said, "Daddy, I asked God to help us, and we are going to get this fixed somehow." That simple child-like faith strengthened my own faith and prayer.

God answered those prayers by giving me an idea. I could not repair the broken fuel line or the broken strap that held the tank in place with only the pliers and screwdriver in the car. I asked Bruce to cut a small branch from a tree. We trimmed it down to plug up the hole from the gas tank and stop the waste of fuel. I took off the tank, wrapped it in a blanket to pad it, and tied it to the luggage rack on top of the car.

The gas gauge, among several other things, did not work on this ten-year-old car, and we had not been able to get it fixed. Several times in the past I had run out of gas, and so had gotten in the habit of carrying extra gas in a gallon can mounted in a special box so it would not turn over.

For the first time, I thanked the Lord for a broken gas gauge. The car had a rusty hole in the floorboard between the front and back seats. I thanked God for that, too. I placed the gas can on the back floorboard and rerouted the gas line. It came up, over, and then down into the spout in the can. A question ran through my mind, "Will the fuel pump have enough suction to draw the gas from the can?" There was only one way to find out.

By this time it was dark and raining even harder. We bowed our heads and asked the Lord to make it work. I turned the key. "Chug-chug-chug," it started. "Praise the Lord!" we cried.

It would have been closer to turn around and return to San Gil, but the road was not wide enough. Instead, we continued up the mountain. Each time the gallon was used up we had to refill the can from the tank on top (not an easy job) and start up the mountain again. We finally reached the top and could see the lights of Duitama below. We coasted most of the way down to avoid the tedious job of pouring gas from the tank into the can. We arrived in Duitama about 9:00 P.M. Only one gas station was open. I pulled in, opened the back door, and said to the attendant, "Fill it up!" He did, with about half a gallon. The look on his face seemed to say, "This gringo must be loco!"

With that gallon of gas we were able to make it to Sogamoso, our destination. The next day we found a mechanic to weld the gas tank back in place. We didn't have any more problems the rest of our journey, but you can be sure we didn't take the "short cut" on our return trip!

Yes, God answered the prayers of a missionary family stranded a long way from home. It's great to know His promise, "Lo, I am with you always . . ." is true! However, He is just as pleased to answer the prayers of any of His children—in times of crises **and** comfort. He answers prayer—just because He loves us.

An example of the breathtaking mountain scenery in Colombia. The winding roads—although affording a beautiful view—often created dangerous driving conditions.

A Full-Time Maid? Wow!

When people in the United States learn that missionaries often have maids, an envious look sometimes comes in their eyes. You can almost hear them say, "Boy, I wish *I* had a maid!"

For missionaries, maids are a necessity, not a luxury, however. When goods such as canned or frozen foods are not available and everything has to be made from scratch, it requires someone working full-time just to keep the household going. For room and board and about a dollar a day, we had a full-time, live-in maid. She could do the time-consuming household tasks and leave Evelyn free to be fully involved in missionary activities.

Another reason in much of the world, including Colombia, for having a maid is the need for someone to "house-sit" during the day. The threat of thieves is ever present. In spite of all our precautions, including bars on the windows and double locks on the doors, we suffered 15 burglaries that I can recall. Some were minor, others more serious.

Sometimes the maid would turn out to be the thief or the "inside person" cooperating with the thieves. One maid turned out to be a cleptomaniac. We began to miss things and became suspicious of her. On her day off we checked her room and found a number of items hidden under her mattress. When she returned, we asked her about them. She insisted they were things she had bought to take to her mother. We had no doubt, however, when one of the items was a can of squid, not available in Colombia! It had been given to us by a North American family returning to the States. We had never gotten up the nerve to eat it!

In addition to the risk of thievery, we had a difficult time convincing a new, inexperienced maid of the need to do things to protect the family's health. Why did you need to boil the drinking water? Why treat lettuce in iodine water? "I can't see those little amoeba that you say will make you sick," many said. Because we did not grow up in Colombia, we had to take many precautions to guard against illnesses which the Colombians didn't have to take.

Having a maid brought other problems. A friend of ours returned to Colombia after furlough. She brought with her a new skillet with a nonstick coating. When she came home one day, her maid said to her, "Señora, it took me all day, but I finally got all that brown stuff out of the skillet!"

During the years we were in Colombia, we had many different maids. We had a chance to share the good news of Christ with most of them. Some of them opened their hearts to the Word and became believers, like Doña María.

Once, our family was leaving town for a week. Our maid had not been with us long. When we started to leave, I said to her, "You won't be alone. The Lord is here with you." Several years later she visited our church and reminded me of that occasion and what I had said. Then she said, "When you told me that, I thought you were crazy. Now I know what you meant. I am a Christian now and I know that the Lord is with me everywhere I go."

Choosing the Right Spot

From the onset of our work in Bucaramanga we began to dream of a permanent home for the church we would start. The city, with a population of 230,000, had only four non-Catholic churches. We did not want to locate too close to any of them, nor to any of the numerous Catholic churches.

Bucaramanga is a beautiful city located in the Eastern range of the Andes mountains. It is situated 3,200 feet above sea level and only seven degrees north of the equator. You might think it would be hot; however, at this altitude we enjoyed spring-like weather all year round. It was a densely populated city—its people lived on a plateau about three miles long.

Because of this, we could not readily find property large enough on which to build a church. We spotted a nice-sized, vacant lot in the general area where we lived and started our mission. I thought it would be a good location for our future church building. Each time I drove by it, I breathed a prayer, "Lord, please save that lot for us." Not long after spotting it, however, houses began to be built on it. "Lord, why did you let them build on *our* spot?" I asked. I looked for other suitable property. The same thing happened again! I complained even stronger to the Lord. Then I found a third location and even talked to the owner about it. He was a Presbyterian and said he would be happy to sell it to us if we raised the money before someone else bought it.

Our third year on the field attendance at the mission began to outgrow our rented facilities, and we needed a permanent location. Building a church building would require a large amount of funds. Southern Baptists' plan for mission support is quite different from other mission groups. The Cooperative Program supports many different types of ministry: foreign missions; home missions; state missions; seminaries; and more. The Foreign Mission Board receives the largest per-

50

centage. Also, 100 percent of the Lottie Moon Christmas Offering is used in foreign missions. Through these means, thousands of churches, large and small, take part in carrying out Jesus' Great Commission. Also, because of these means, Southern Baptist missionaries do not have to raise their own support. Missionaries from other sending agencies spend a major portion of their time soliciting funds for their work.

Funds for specific projects are requested almost a year in advance and according to priority. When our need for a church building reached top priority, we were granted $25,000 to buy property and begin a long-range building program. I contacted the owner of the third property I had selected and asked him if it was still available. My heart sank when he said no. Again, I asked the Lord why?

I then asked the property owner if he had any other property that might meet our needs. He said, "I have some old houses on 37th Street that might suit you." I remember thinking, I have never seen anything there that could be adequate, but it won't hurt to look. I met him at the property at the appointed time. As it turned out, it was several very old houses that had been converted into a factory for making cement floor tile. The factory had been closed about a year—almost to the day that our request for funds had been moved up on the priority list! As the owner unlocked the door, the Lord spoke within my heart. "Here is your property!" It turned out to be a much better location than any of the others I had selected, only six blocks from the center of town.

This property was on a corner, facing a park. (Bucaramanga is known as "The City of Parks.") In fact, it was the only major park in the city without a Catholic church facing it! As I looked at it, Isaiah 55:8-9 came to mind: "'For My thoughts are not your thoughts, Neither are your ways My ways,' declares the Lord. 'For as the heavens are higher than the earth, So are My ways higher than your ways, and My thoughts than your thoughts'" (NASB). I asked the Lord to forgive me for complaining about not saving "my" properties!

Beginning to Build

After purchasing the property, we had $15,000 to use for construction. I selected an architect and explained what we had in mind. The church would have to be built in stages, since money was limited. We wanted a sanctuary, or auditorium, that would seat about 350 people. We also needed classrooms for the different Sunday School classes. The architect was a Catholic; he had never heard of Sunday School. Also, he could not understand the type of baptistry we needed. In his church the baptistry was something like a large bird bath. I explained ours was something like a small swimming pool. I explained to him baptism by immersion and what it symbolized. We finally came up with an acceptable plan.

I hired young men (including one of Doña María's sons) to begin demolition of the old houses in the area where the sanctuary would be constructed. We saved as much as possible of the houses outside that area to serve as Sunday School classrooms. The houses were about 100 years old. The walls were 18 inches thick and made of "rammed earth," a popular way of constructing homes. Wooden forms 18 inches apart had been set on top of a foundation of large rocks. Dirt was slightly moistened, placed between the forms and rammed (packed) firmly with a wooden pole. A few days later, when it was dry, the forms were moved higher and the process repeated until the walls were as high as needed. The dirt cost nothing and labor was cheap. The thick walls made the houses stay cool all day. The roof was made of Spanish tile, also effective in keeping the tropical heat out. Then the walls were plastered with a mixture of mud and cow manure—more inexpensive material! The manure gave it a texture that repelled the rain. The walls were then whitewashed. This process seems strange to us today, but remember, they had lasted about 100 years and could have lasted another 100 if properly maintained.

Soon after the Corleys began missions work in Colombia, they dreamed of a permanent church home. In 1967, work began on First Baptist Church, Bucaramanga. By Easter, this much was completed. Although it was only partially finished, the members were thankful to finally have a church home.

The finished First Baptist Church, Bucaramanga.

The architect's plans for the church were finally finished and approved by the Mission and the city. I was ready to get started on the building. Our furlough was scheduled to start only seven months away, and I wanted to get at least the sanctuary completed before we left. I contacted several contractors and asked if they could construct the building by July. Each said it would be impossible. The contractor I was most impressed with said, "As you know, most of the month of December and the first week of January are holidays. If I start now, I would have to pay the workmen for those holidays even though they don't work."

"If I get my crew to dig the foundation and have it ready to begin pouring concrete on January 8, can you finish it by July?" I asked.

"Yes, I think I can," he answered.

I like a "can do" spirit and hired him.

Edgar A. Guest wrote a poem, "It Couldn't Be Done," which has been helpful to me when faced with a difficult task. The first verse says:

Somebody said that it couldn't be done,
    But he with a chuckle replied
That "maybe it couldn't," but he would be one
    Who wouldn't say so till he'd tried.
So he buckled right in with the trace of a grin
    On his face. If he worried he hid it.
He started to sing as he tackled the thing
    That couldn't be done, and he did it.[1]

I composed a melody for it and have sung it many times, usually to myself, when things seemed impossible.

When I met with Dr. Chávez, the contractor I had chosen, to sign the contract, I said, "Dr. Chávez, I consider this job as the Lord's work. Let's pray and ask the Lord to bless our efforts." He agreed. I bowed my head and began to pray. To my surprise, he began to repeat each word I said. Here was a grown man, a graduate engineer, who considered himself a Christian, yet he probably had never prayed except by repeating the words of someone else.

The young men I hired for the demolition had no experience in construction. I knew another man who was knowledgeable of construction, although he had had no formal training. He had just "picked it up" working with others. He could "read" a blueprint, although he could barely read a book. He and I began to lay out the foundations for the sanctuary and one small section of classrooms. I learned many simple methods from him I had not learned in engineering and construction in the US.

When we had the building "laid out," I hired another man to help dig the foundations. The construction would be reinforced concrete columns and beams strong enough to withstand earthquakes. The footing for each column was about 6-by-6 feet, and the holes were 8 to 10 feet deep. The sanctuary alone had 22 columns. In digging, we reached clay called "sangre de torro" (blood of a bull, as it is called). This clay is so hard that when a sharp pointed heavy steel bar is dropped on it, the bar falls over rather than sticks into the ground. All digging was done with pick and shovel. The dirt was hauled away in wheelbarrows. This was a lot of hard work, but these four men got it done. On January 8, Chávez's crew began shaping steel reinforcement bars and pouring concrete.

All the concrete and mortar had to be mixed by hand. All cutting of wood for the forms, columns, and beams had to be done with a handsaw. The bricks were large, about the size of five American bricks. Materials were raised by handing buckets to levels higher than the workers' heads. When levels got too high, they used a pulley and rope to raise the buckets. It was a slow process but he had a large number of workers so we could see progress from day to day.

I have been an inventor since I was a child. When the walls became very high, especially on the facade, I used my four-wheel drive vehicle to make an elevator. I jacked up the rear wheels and right front tire, replacing it with an empty rim. This served as a drum to wind up the rope, and it raised more materials faster than could be done by hand.

Easter and Christmas are the two most important times for Christians. This is especially true in Catholic countries. As Easter approached, church members said they would like to have the special services in the new building, even though it was not finished. By then we had only about three-fourths of the walls built and one-half of the roof on. Churches in America would not even think of having services in a partially finished building, but these people were thankful to God for their new church home!

We did get the sanctuary almost completed before leaving for furlough that year. At the same time, the church members called a Colombian pastor, which left us free to consider other places of service beyond Bucaramanga when we returned from furlough. Even today, however, the building does not have a ceiling in it (one can look up and see the underside of the roof). The balcony has never been completed, either. This doesn't make sense to us in America, but remember, these are poor people who are not accustomed to what Americans consider necessities. Instead of completing the sanctuary, they have borrowed money from the Colombian Baptist Convention Loan Board in order to build more classrooms. They consider classrooms a more urgent need than a ceiling. Remember, churches are not buildings, they are people.

[1]Reprinted from THE COLLECTED VERSES OF EDGAR A. GUEST. Copyright 1934, Contemporary Books, Inc. Used with permission by CONTEMPORARY BOOKS, INC.

A New Broom Sweeps Clean

As the title of this book suggests, Doña María wasn't the only Colombian who became dear friends to us. The "Friends" refer to the many brothers and sisters in Christ we met in Colombia. The old adage, "Any friend of yours is a friend of mine," was certainly true there. Doña María did not know all the people we knew; however, she always had a deep interest in anyone pertaining to us or the Lord's work.

One of the friends she did know well was David González. David, like Doña María, was in the first group of believers to be baptized. David made brooms and brushes for a living. He owned his own "factory," which was in his home; he was also the "sales force" for his products. His wife and older children worked with him.

David's "factory" consisted of a homemade combination saw/drill. The saw was mounted on one end of an axle, which was mounted in ball bearings. The drill was on the other extreme of the axle. This allowed one motor to operate both machines.

The saw was used to cut various sized blocks of wood. David then drilled holes in the blocks to place the brushes' bristles in. The bristles were either broom straw, fibers from vines, or second-hand plastic box strapping, cut into strips. The smaller brushes were made for hand use. The larger ones, for scrubbing floors, needed a handle. To do that, David bored a hole in the block of wood at the proper angle. A special tool was used to cut threads in this hole. Another special tool was used to make threads on the end of a broomstick. The handle was then screwed into the block. The fibers were bunched together with a piece of wire doubled over them. These were then driven into rows of small holes with a hammer and a special punch.

Household brooms were made in a different manner. Like

the others, however, the machine for making them was also homemade.

David's factory was located in one small room and patio adjoining two other rooms and a kitchen. (These two rooms were their living quarters.) David and his family shared the house with four other families who lived and worked there, also. The house was old and made from adobe bricks. It covered the entire lot, except for two patios. The lot was about 50 feet wide and 100 feet deep. The house had a garage, but none of the residents owned a car, so one man had converted it into a shoe factory/repair shop. The other three families had a joint venture making cigars. They were hand-made but were not like fine Havana cigars. They were the "tobaccos" which Doña María smoked. The house had only one bathroom for all 40 residents.

David was first in his family to become a Christian. His wife was a strong Catholic and wanted nothing to do with his new-found faith. She didn't even come to see him baptized. However, as God began to transform David's life, she began to think that maybe Evangelicals weren't so bad after all. She began to attend the church, and after accepting the Lord, she became a faithful worker in the church, working with GAs, an organization for girls in the church. She even became president of the Woman's Missionary Union, a missions organization for women and girls.

When we started the demolition of the houses on the permanent church property, David and his family became the caretakers. He set up his factory in a back corner. After the church was built, he continued to serve as caretaker, custodian, and guard. In that capacity he witnessed to people who came asking for help, which was frequently.

About ten years later he moved his family to Medellín, and we had only limited contact with him. Occasionally he would return to Bucaramanga on business. On one such trip he was to return to Medellín by bus as far as Barranca, cross the Magdalena River, and take the train to Medellín. When I found out his travel plans, I said, "I will be driving to Barranca tomorrow afternoon. Why don't you come to our house, have lunch with us, and then ride to Barranca with me?" He was happy with the idea. It would give us time together and save him bus fare, too.

When he came, we shared a sweet time of fellowship. He told us news of his family as we sat around the table. I had not been feeling well that morning, and so I said to him, "I think it may be wise for me to postpone my trip until I am feeling better."

"That is no problem," he said. "I'll just go by bus as I had planned." After lunch, Evelyn drove him to the bus station and he caught the 2:30 P.M. bus.

As we were eating supper that evening, the phone rang. A young man from the church said, "I just heard on the radio that a bus wrecked just out of town. It said a Catholic nun and a man named David González were killed. Do you think it might be our David?" He and I went to the morgue and, yes, it was our David. I grieved deeply, not only from losing a dear friend but from guilt. I thought, "If I had gone on as planned, this would not have happened!"

I called his family in Medellín and shared the sad news with them. We had his body embalmed so it could be transported. (In Colombia, most corpses are not embalmed because of the cost and must be buried within 24 hours.) The next day, I accompanied his body to Medellín. It was a sad occasion for all as we laid him to rest, yet we had a calm assurance we would see him again, in a far more beautiful place!

On several occasions David had said, "When my time comes I hope I die quickly." God honored his request!

Bibles at a Fair

A state fair is held in Bucaramanga each year. While Wilson Donehoo was director of the Baptist Book Store in Bogotá, I helped him build a portable booth display for books which could be used at such occasions. We used the booth two years in Bucaramanga displaying and selling Bibles and Christian books. During one state fair we gave away more than 37,000 booklets of the Gospel of Luke, published by the American Bible Society, as well as sold Bible Society Bibles and Catholic Bibles.

We watched the different reactions of people with interest. Some would receive the Gospel of Luke booklet gladly with a warm, "Thank you!" Some would take one just because it was free. Others would respond, "No, thank you," and still others would take the booklet and open it to the title page to see if it contained an official note of approval from the Catholic church. Since it didn't, they would give it back. Outside the booth, we would find some of the booklets torn up and thrown on the ground.

During the week, a woman and her daughter dropped by the booth. The daughter studied at one of the most prominent Catholic schools in the city, and she told us the nuns who taught there had told the students, "Be careful that you don't read any of those false Gospels they are giving away at the fair." This young girl's teacher told them, "Friday I will give a prize to the student who brings the most booklets, and we will tear them up in class!"

We placed a box at one end of the booth's counter containing some of the torn up copies we had picked up around the stand. I made a sign for the box which read, "Father, forgive them; for they know not what they do."

One afternoon a priest came by and began to rebuke the young man, Carlos, who was tending the booth. "Why are you

Protestants selling these 'false Bibles'?" he asked. Carlos picked up a Bible Society Bible and another Bible which was approved by the Catholic church. It also contained footnotes explaining Catholic theology. We were selling that version for persons who preferred it. Carlos said to the priest, "Father, I will tell you why. Ours sells for 50 pesos and yours costs 200 pesos! The reason you are mad is that you don't want people to read the Bible. They will learn that much of what you teach is not true!"

By this time a crowd had gathered. Carlos reached into the box containing the torn-up copies, picked up a handful, and held them in front of the priest's face. "You should ask God to forgive you for teaching the people to destroy His Word!" he exclaimed.

The priest was speechless. He turned and walked away. The crowd moved in closer and began asking questions, and several bought Bibles.

Jesus said, "A sower went forth to sow . . ." (see Matt. 13:3-8 KJV). We saw some seed sprout and bear fruit. Others didn't.

At the time, we were renting a house for our worship services. One Saturday afternoon I went there to make preparations for the services the next day. When I unlocked the front door, I spotted one of the Gospels of Luke on the floor. It had been set afire! Had someone tried to burn the church? The building was constructed of brick and concrete, so it wouldn't burn. The door was made of wood, but showed no sign of damage. Regardless, it was an extreme rejection of what we were trying to do. I must confess, it shook me up! What else might someone try to do? I thumbed through the burned pages. Suddenly these words leaped off the page, "Be not afraid of them that kill the body, and after that have no more that they can do" (Luke 12:4 KJV).

A Father Who Became a Brother

We had been serving in Colombia about three years when I began hearing about a certain Catholic priest in Bogotá. His name was Reverend Father Rafael García Herreros, but he was affectionately known as Padre García Herreros. He began a program to help poor families have a modest home and a good education. He named the area Minuto de Dios.

Padre García Herreros also encouraged people to read the Bible. At the time, Catholics in Colombia were not encouraged to read the Bible. In fact, our Spanish tutor told us that as a young man he had been preparing for the priesthood. He abandoned the idea about three years before he was to be ordained. To that point he still had not held a Bible in his hands. We gave him his first Bible.

One Baptist pastor in Bogotá knew Padre García Herreros, and he introduced us. The priest learned I was a Baptist missionary, and after we had talked a few minutes, he abruptly said, "Mario, I am a Roman Catholic. I don't want you to try to make a Baptist out of me!"

I replied, "Sir, I am as much a Baptist as you are a Catholic. I don't want you to try to make a Catholic out of me. What I want is for you and me to dedicate ourselves to teaching the people of Colombia that Christ is not on the cross. He is alive and seated victoriously at the right hand of the Father!"

Padre García Herreros replied, "I agree with that!" That statement became the basis of our friendship.

That same day as we walked about his neighborhood, he said, "Mario, each Saturday some other priests and I go on an outing to read the Bible and pray. I would like for you to go with us."

I said, "I would like that very much. I must return to Bucaramanga tomorrow, but the next time I come to Bogotá I will plan to be here on a Saturday."

I returned to Bogotá later and joined him and the other priests on their outing. We went to an Eudist seminary near Bogotá, the religious order under which he served. Four priests were present, including the director of the seminary. We talked for about three hours, discussing several things: the Bible; social issues; the mission Christ left the church. In the process, I shared my personal testimony of what God had done in my life.

When time came for lunch, they said, "We are going to the chapel for our noontime prayers. Would you like to go with us?" I replied that I would. While they read from their prayer book, I sat and prayed silently.

During lunch, Padre García Herreros said to me, "Mario, I would like for you to come on my television program and tell the people of Colombia what you told us this morning."

I was dumbfounded. I replied, "I appreciate the invitation, but I don't think my Spanish is good enough to speak on television."

"I don't think that will be a problem," he said. "I want the people to hear you." I told him I needed some time to pray about it and I would let him know later.

After lunch we went outside. A small lake with an island sat on the seminary's campus, with the island connected to the campus by a footbridge. We walked across the bridge and sat on the island, under the warm sun. The priests read some Scripture verses and a prayer from their prayer book. When they finished, I asked, "May I read some Scripture and pray?"

They replied, "Certainly." I proceeded to read some verses from Romans, then I prayed as I had learned from my youth, telling the Lord what I felt in my heart. When I finished, Padre García Herreros said to the other priests, "Wouldn't it be wonderful if we could learn to pray from our hearts, like that!" I am glad to say that in the following years I witnessed him do just that. He and I shared many precious times on our knees, telling God what was on our hearts.

As I prayed about the invitation to appear on television, I was hesitant to accept it. No other non-Catholic minister had ever spoken on the program. Would it have a negative impact on our Baptist work? Would it compromise our Scriptural position? I asked, "Lord, please show me what You want me to do!" He helped me see that it was an opportunity to speak to millions of people to whom I would never be able to speak otherwise.

The program, "El Minuto de Dios" (God's Minute), was actually five minutes of prime time, just after the evening news. Colombia had only one TV channel at that time and about eight million people watched the program each night.

The Lord blessed the message that night. I did not have to compromise my convictions in any way. He also gave me the opportunity, on future occasions, to speak on subjects such as "Jesus, the Good Shepherd," "The Word of God in Your Life," "Jesus and Zacchaeus," "The Holy Spirit in Our Lives," "Spiritual Milk," and others. Padre García Herreros said to me, "Say what the Lord places on your heart. All I ask is, don't get me in trouble with the cardinal. I have enough complaints from him already."

God blessed my efforts each time. On other occasions that grew out of this friendship I had numerous contacts with people in high places, giving me opportunities to share the good news with them.

Padre García Herreros and I did not agree on everything, but I learned from him and he learned from me. I remember one delicate point we discussed. Roman Catholics pray to the Virgin Mary. They believe that she was not only a virgin when Jesus was born, but she remained a virgin the rest of her life.

The question that I was asked more than any other during my ministry in Colombia was, "Do you believe in the Virgin?" I learned to answer, "I believe everything the Bible says about the virgin." I learned that if I said no, the person did not hear a word I said after that. If they really wanted to know more about what the Bible said, they would ask further questions and we could help them understand.

We heard the expression "Mary, the Mother of God" often in Colombia. The Colombians reasoned, "Jesus is God. Mary is Jesus' mother. Therefore, she is the Mother of God." If the person was spiritually mature enough to consider the subject, I tried to help them understand the following: Christ-Jesus was God-Man, divine-human. God was His Heavenly Father. Mary was His earthly mother. Mary was not the mother of God. God does not have a mother. She would have to be eternal to be His mother. This would call for a "quadrinity," rather than the Trinity the Bible teaches.

During one discussion with Padre García Herreros, I commented that we did not regard Mary as being on the same level as God, nor did we pray to her. I cited Isaiah 42:8, "I am the Lord, that is My name: and I will not give My glory to another" (NASB).

He replied, "Not even to His mother?"

"Not even to His mother!"

Through the years we experienced many wonderful things together through our common Sonship with the Lord. I used the term *Padre* in speaking to him only in situations where it would have been awkward for him among his parishioners. To me he was not a Father, he was a brother!

Bibles at a Banquet

Padre García Herreros was a very compassionate person. His heart was deeply moved by the abject poverty in which so many people of Colombia live, and he did something about it. Around 1960 he began a program of enlisting wealthy people to build homes for families who had none or who lived in pitiful conditions. He organized what he called the "Banquet of the Million" to raise a million pesos to build these homes. It became an annual affair. Through the years he accomplished more than anyone ever dreamed possible. He developed a subdivision in Bogotá of more than 2,000 homes. The subdivision includes a complete school system, offering quality education from pre-school through high school, a seminary, and a university. The subdivision offers job training, arts and crafts classes, and many other self-help programs. It includes a Catholic church, but also an art museum and a theater which shows only wholesome pictures. The subdivision has set high moral standards. If a person or family violates these standards, they are asked to leave, their home reverts to the community, and it is sold to another family willing to assume their place. It is the only place in Bogotá where you dare to leave your car unlocked. The name of the barrio, or subdivision, is Minuto de Dios (after the television program of the same name). The name and what it stands for are known throughout the country and beyond.

In 1971 I was visiting with Padre García Herreros a few days before the annual banquet. Tickets were equivalent to $500. His goal was 1,000 people in attendance. Some individuals and companies made generous contributions, over and above the ticket fee. As we were chatting, the padre said, "Mario, I would like for you to attend the banquet as my guest." I was overwhelmed. I told him I was honored and would consider it. I really wanted time to pray, to know if the

Lord wanted me to attend. We walked from his office to his home.

A friend of mine in Bucaramanga, a member of the Gideons, had asked me to see if there was any possibility of giving New Testaments to the people who would be attending the banquet. As we stood in his doorway, I asked, "My brother, if I can come to the banquet, what would you think of giving a New Testament to each person who attends?"

Without uttering a word, he spun on his heels, walked into his living room, sat down on the couch, put his arm on the back of the couch, and buried his face in his arm. He sat deep in thought for a long moment. Suddenly he raised his head and said, "Mario, let's try it. You know that the Catholics of Colombia have not been taught to appreciate the Bible. Some who come to the banquet are Jews. They won't have much interest in the New Testament. Some who come are Communists. They don't care for the Bible at all! But, let's see what happens!" I replied, "Remember, my brother, I do not know yet if I can come. I will do what I can."

My immediate thought was, I didn't have 1,000 New Testaments! My Gideon friend in Bucaramanga didn't have them either. I called another friend, the president of the Gideon Camp in Bogotá. He had access to that many copies, but he didn't think Gideon policy would let them be distributed at a fund-raising project in which they were not involved. "What do I do now, Lord?" I asked in desperation. I flew back to Bucaramanga that afternoon. I had preaching responsibilities there on Sunday. Every moment from then on was bathed in prayer. "Father, show me Your will. If this is what You want me to do, please let me know." Church members were praying, also. The more I prayed, the more I was convinced that He had planted the idea in our hearts. Still, the banquet was only three days away.

Then the Lord brought to mind something I had been told while on furlough; perhaps here was the answer. Our home church, Lakeside Baptist Church of Dallas, Texas, had told me, "Marion, if you have a special need that we can help you with, just let us know." I did not have enough time to contact them, however. I would have to hope that they would see this endeavor, which would cost several hundred dollars, as something they could do. If not, the expense would have to come out of my pocket.

I ordered 1,000 Spanish New Testaments from the American Bible Society in Bogotá. I also purchased a nice, leather-bound Bible and had the name of the president of Colombia, Dr. Misael Pastrana Borrero, printed in gold on the front cover. I asked an artist friend to prepare a parchment to be placed inside the Bible. It read:

King David said:
"Thy word is a lamp unto my feet, and a light unto
my path."
Psalms 119:105 (KJV)

May the wisdom of God guide your steps.
May the love of God fill your heart.
May the Word of God be your inspiration.

I returned to Bogotá the day before the banquet. It was to be held at the city's finest hotel. Several hours before the banquet began, I placed a New Testament at each plate. I purposely saved about half of the boxes and placed them behind a curtain, out of sight. They would be useful for carrying home New Testaments left behind, I thought.

One thousand places were set, each with a small loaf of bread, a commemorative wine glass, and a New Testament. As the guests arrived, I noticed many prominent business people, political leaders, TV stars, and other well-known persons. Most of them would have never been accessible to me normally. At the head table sat the mayor of Bogotá, high ranking military leaders, and President Pastrana. Miss Colombia served their table. Padre García Herreros welcomed everyone and expressed appreciation for their presence and help. He told about his dream of helping not only the needy of Bogotá, but also in other areas of Colombia. President Pastrana thanked him profusely for helping the poor and hungry. As the people enjoyed the "meal" (it was only the bread and wine), I approached the head table and presented the president with his Bible. He was very cordial and expressed his appreciation for it. The encounter paved the way for me to visit the Presidential Palace on several occasions.

When the banquet was over, I went from table to table to collect the New Testaments left behind. I could not find even one! People treasured anything as a souvenir from this prestigious occasion. Many, no doubt, took theirs home and put it on a shelf to gather dust. Even so, sometime later in a time of grief or special need, perhaps they read it and came to know the truth of the Living Word. Only eternity will show the final results.

Fortunately, Lakeside Baptist Church was happy to pay for the New Testaments. In the years that followed, we distributed New Testaments or Bibles on other occasions. The Gideons provided them in the years we did not. In other years, we knew of occasions ahead of time and included the cost in our budget planning. These occasions put me in contact with four different presidents and brought about numerous opportunities to share with leaders of Colombia on many levels. It also gave me contacts which proved to be important.

A humorous incident happened the next time we presented Bibles at the banquet. We had printed a special certificate to be pasted in the flyleaf of each New Testament. It was John 20:31: "But these things are written, that ye might believe that Jesus is the Christ, the Son of God; and that believing ye might have life through His name" (KJV). For the pasting we enlisted the help of young people from Minuto de Dios. I carried the boxes there two days before the banquet.

The day of the banquet I went to pick them up. As I bent down to pick up a box, I heard a "r-i-i-i-p." To my horror, I had ripped the seam in my pants! I found Padre García Herreros and said, "What am I going to do now?"

He said, "Don't worry. Come with me." He took me upstairs, gave me his bathrobe, and said, "Let me have your pants." In a few minutes he came back with my pants neatly mended. I may be the only Baptist missionary in history who had the seam of his pants sewn up by a Catholic nun!

Hitting Straight with a Crooked Stick

We returned to Colombia in 1968 after our first year of furlough. Pastor Ricaurte, who became pastor of the church before we left for furlough, had worked hard while we were gone and the Lord had blessed his efforts; the church had grown considerably. We soon began to think of how we could extend a Baptist witness into other parts of our area.

Not long after we returned, we had an unexpected visit from a man named Víctor Sánchez and a group of new believers from Cúcuta, the capital city of North Santander. They wanted our church to sponsor them as a mission. Several were baptized while they were in Bucaramanga.

As we came to know Víctor, we were immediately impressed with his personality. He could be very convincing. A born leader, he was also very intelligent. He was an experienced nurse, licensed by the government to practice and teach nursing. He had organized a group of women and was teaching them the basics of health care. His goal was to train them to serve as midwives among the poor who could not afford medical care. I sometimes jokingly called him a mid-husband, for he delivered many babies himself.

Víctor was also a good musician. He played the accordion well and led groups in singing songs and choruses that deeply stirred their hearts and attracted new people.

However, when we asked pastors from other parts of the country about him, we discovered he did not have a good reputation. He had worked in several cities and had left a trail of problems. Pastor Ricaurte and I asked him about his reputation. He answered, "Brothers, what you heard about my past is true. I will not deny any of it. But I am a different man now. I am married, have one child, and another on the way. I only ask you for a chance to prove myself." We were impressed with his attitude and desire to correct a questionable past.

I visited the mission in Cúcuta as frequently as possible. It was a joy to be with them, for their spirit was contagious. They met in the small home of a very poor family. Their singing would "raise the roof," as we say in America. Víctor's preaching was always biblical. New people were being reached every Sunday. Before long, they had to find a larger place to meet. Things were going great.

Suddenly Víctor and his family moved to Bucaramanga. He said the hot climate of Cúcuta was causing his wife unbearable suffering, since her baby was overdue. I preached the following Sunday at the mission in Cúcuta. After the service, I took some of the members home. After dropping them off, I started to the hotel where I was staying. A man who lived on the same street as the people I had dropped off flagged me down. He asked, "Are you the Baptist missionary?"

I said, "Yes, I am."

He replied, "Please come into my house for a few minutes." Once inside, he said, "I think you need to know the kind of man you are working with." He proceeded to tell me that his daughter had been one of Víctor's nursing students. She had become very ill, and Víctor had told them she had appendicitis and needed to go to the hospital for an operation immediately. When her parents saw her being rolled out of the obstetrics operating room, they asked the surgeon, "Why was she in there for an appendectomy?"

The doctor had replied, "She did not have appendicitis. She was pregnant, had an abortion, and a very serious infection almost caused her death."

The girl's father then told me, "Víctor got her pregnant, did the abortion, and tried to cover it up. So you will know all this is true, I want my daughter to confirm it." He called her into the room. She was very pale and weak. The father, point by point, reviewed what he had told me and asked her, "Is this true?" She, with her head hung in humiliation said, "Yes, that is the truth."

Her father said, "I am a believer, but I hate that man! If it

would not cause a scandal, I would take my gun and kill him!'"
No wonder Víctor had left town suddenly.

You can imagine that this knowledge caused some of the
new converts to doubt what Víctor had preached. Some of
them turned away, saying, "If he is living a lie, his message
must be false, also." Christ said, "But whoever causes one of
these little ones who believe in Me to stumble, it is better for
him that a heavy millstone be hung around his neck and that
he be drowned into the depth of the sea" (Matt. 18:6 NASB).
God will settle the account with Víctor and those like him.
At the same time, all of us must be careful with the testimony
we bear. If we could see our own hearts, as God sees us, we
might find attitudes of pride, self righteousness, or rebellion
that make God just as sad.

Not long after, missionary Jimmy Stiles came to live and
work in Cúcuta and the surrounding area. He helped these
young Christians grow and reach out to others. He often said,
"God can hit straight with a crooked stick." As unfortunate as
Víctor's scandalous conduct was, the people who were following Christ rather than Víctor still came to rejoice in the
changing power of the gospel. It is the message, not the mes-
senger, that transforms lives!

Jimmy was able to help these new believers develop indi-
vidually and as a group. They rented a building in a central location for their worship center. Later, Lottie Moon Christmas
Offering funds helped them purchase property and build the
first unit of their church building. After four years, Jimmy and
his family moved to Bogotá, but while they were in Cúcuta
they made a lasting contribution to the area. During our 22
years in Colombia that was the only time we had other Southern Baptist missionaries in our area.

The Lord has blessed the efforts of the Colombians them-
selves, and many have come to know Him. Colombia suffers
from an acute shortage of pastors. Sometimes a church has a
pastor; other times members carry the full load of ministry.
When a church is without a pastor, it names members to serve

as an administrative committee. This committee shares in and assigns the preaching and other responsibilities. They have even started preaching points and other missions in Cúcuta and the surrounding areas. Through the years I have noticed that God can use people who, humanly speaking, don't have much to offer. Their greatest ability is availability. He can even hit straight with a crooked stick!

Ministry Through Music

Music is magical—it can open the hearts of people everywhere. Often the Mission office in Colombia would receive inquiries from Southern Baptist church choirs who wanted to tour Colombia. Groups which wanted just to "tour and sing" took up valuable missionary time, which was already overbooked. If, however, groups wanted to "work and minister," we had much they could do. Even so, we received more requests than we could handle.

It took a lot of time and effort to plan and coordinate such events, then serve as guide and interpreter. However, I loved good music and saw unlimited possibilities for sharing the gospel with it. Through music we could enter areas we could never reach through preaching or other conventional methods. During the time we served in Colombia, I coordinated five different choir tours. Some groups sang on nationwide TV, others at the Presidential Palace, Congress, Catholic churches and schools, parks, airports, military bases, and jails, as well as Baptist churches.

One thing I insisted on was that groups *must* learn to sing in Spanish. It is much easier to sing in another language than to speak it. If members could speak some as well, that was even better. You've probably heard the expression, "Music is a universal language," and that is true. You can entertain people through music without understanding the words. However, you can't communicate the gospel if the audience can't understand what's being sung!

I also sent each group a choral arrangement of the Colombian national anthem. We always opened each concert with it. That melted a lot of ice!

Just in Time

In 1972 the choir from South Main Baptist Church, Houston, Texas, came to Colombia for concerts in several cities. I had offered to help them plan and carry out their activities. One of the places I had scheduled them to sing was in the barrio Minuto de Dios.

When I met the group at the airport in Bogotá, the director, Thad Roberts, said to me, "Marion, I brought a box of 50 Spanish New Testaments. Can you use them?"

I replied, "Yes. I don't know where right now, but we can always put them to good use."

When we arrived at Minuto de Dios that afternoon, Padre García Herreros greeted us and said, "Mario, can you get me 50 New Testaments?"

Amazed, I replied, "Yes, I can. Why do you need them?"

He responded, "Some of my seminary students are going out into the rural areas during school vacation, two by two as Jesus sent the disciples, to visit house to house and share the gospel with the people. When they find a family that shows interest and does not have a Bible, I would like to leave a New Testament for them to read."

I said, "Yes, my brother, I have your New Testaments!"

I did not have them with me at the moment. They were in my jeep and I had come on the bus with the choir. However, I did not think time was a major factor, since school vacation in Bucaramanga was still several months off.

The concert was presented to a very responsive crowd, and the choir was elated at the reaction of the people both during the concert and in a time of sharing afterwards. Thad told me that he wanted to return there with his camera to take some pictures. I thought we could do that anytime before we left Bogotá.

The following day I was showing the choir some of the

Thad Roberts and Marion Corley arrived at Padre García Herreros' just in time to give semi-nary students Spanish New Testaments. Padre García Herreros is standing third from left.

sights of the city, Baptist work in particular. We were at the building site of Trinity Baptist Church when, suddenly, I felt a strong impulse to go to Minuto de Dios. I said to Thad, "Let's go take the pictures you mentioned." He agreed, and we headed there in my jeep while the other choir members returned to the hotel.

When we arrived at Minuto de Dios, Padre García Herreros was pacing back and forth in front of the church. As I pulled up, he said, "Mario, I'm so glad to see you. I thought you wouldn't make it in time."

"What do you mean?" I asked.

"The students are packing their knapsacks, getting ready

to leave without the New Testaments," he answered.

Our school vacation was later in the year, and I thought the trip would take place then. Fortunately, the box of New Testaments was in the back of my jeep, and the young men were able to take them as planned. We prayed together and they left. I was thankful that I had heeded the impulse that surely had come from the Lord. When we get to heaven, it will be interesting to meet the people who found Christ through those New Testaments and visits.

One of my favorite passages from the Bible is found in Proverbs 3:5-6: "Trust in the Lord with all thine heart; and lean not unto thine own understanding. In all thy ways acknowledge him, and he shall direct thy paths" (KJV).

Singing on TV

The contacts I made through appearing on the "Minuto de Dios" television program opened many doors. One result was that when a choir came to Colombia, I could usually arrange for them to sing on TV.

The choir from South Main Baptist Church, Houston, was one such group. They had learned the National Anthem of Colombia and sang it very well. I suggested, "Thad, what do you think of opening with the Colombian anthem? We could follow it with "The Star Spangled Banner." I think I can get flags and a color guard to represent each country."

Thad responded, "Sounds good to me!"

I called the United States Embassy and asked if it could provide a flag and Marines for the occasion. The person I spoke with thought the action would help strengthen the friendship between the two countries and agreed to do so. "Just tell me when and where they are to go," he said.

Next, I called the office of the commander of the Colombian army. I explained to the officer in charge what we wanted to do. "I'll see what can be done," he replied.

When the day arrived, we went to the TV station to tape the program. The Marines were already present, looking sharp. However, the Colombian guard was nowhere in sight. We waited a while; Colombians are not known for punctuality. The TV crew was about ready to roll. I decided to call the commander's office to see if the guard was on its way.

An official answered my call. "This is Reverend Corley speaking," I said.

"Si, Padre." (He thought I was a priest. I didn't correct him.)

"A choir of gringos (foreigners) is here at the TV station. They want to sing the Colombian national anthem and the American national anthem. American Marines are here to serve as color guard for the US flag, but the color guard for the Colombian flag has not arrived. It sure will look bad if we don't have one!"

"Just a moment, Padre." After a long pause, he said, "Padre, the commander says that he will have one there in 15 minutes. Please ask them to wait."

The base was not far from the station, and they were there in about 12 minutes. They were not as "spit and polished" as the Marines, but their participation avoided embarrassment to everyone.

My contacts opened doors not only to choirs. When Owen Cooper was president of the Southern Baptist Convention, I mentioned him to Padre García Herreros. The priest said, "I wish he could encourage our people to live for Christ as he does."

Shortly after that, Cooper made a videotape that was later broadcast on "Minuto de Dios."

One day as the priest and I were talking, he said to me, "Mario, can you get Billy Graham to speak on 'Minuto de Dios'?"

"I don't know, but we can try," I answered.

I wrote to Graham's office and extended the invitation. His office responded that Graham was already overextended and his doctor had ordered him to limit his activities. I shared this with the priest, and he understood.

Ironically, 15 years previous to this Graham had held a crusade in Colombia and experienced strong opposition from the Catholic church.

We also had opportunity for a Colombian Baptist choir to sing on TV, and they made a strong impact on many of the station's personnel.

A Cancelled Concert

The youth choir from the Wieuca Road Baptist Church, Atlanta, toured Colombia in 1979. Before they arrived, a friend of mine, Carlos, suggested that we schedule them to sing at St. Peter's Catholic Church, located in an affluent part of town. Carlos, a Presbyterian and an active Gideon, knew the priests who taught in the school at St. Peter's. I told him, "If you can arrange it, fine. It will be an opportunity to share with a lot of people whom we couldn't reach otherwise." Carlos was able to make the arrangements, and it became part of the itinerary.

I met the choir in Bogotá. They sang in several places there, including the Presidential Palace and on nationwide TV. When we arrived in Bucaramanga, Carlos called me to say, "I'm sorry to tell you this, but the concert for tonight has been cancelled," he said.

"Why?" I asked.

"As I understand it, the bishop is against it."

"Then let's go talk to him and see what the problem is."

The bishop and I had known each other for several years and were pretty good friends. After we had chatted a few minutes, I said, "I understand you have cancelled tonight's concert. May I ask why?"

"Marion, let me be frank with you," he said.

"Please do," I answered.

"It seems like proselytizing for a Baptist choir to sing in one of my churches."

"Sir, here is a copy of the program. As you can see, the name *Baptist* doesn't appear on it anywhere. What if you introduced them as 'a group of Christian young people from Atlanta, Georgia'?"

"That sounds fine with me," he said.

"I hope you can come hear them sing," I said.

"I'm afraid it wouldn't be prudent for me to be there."

Carlos and I expressed our thanks and left immediately to tell the choir the concert was still on. It would begin in only three hours.

I had never met the parochial priest (pastor) of this church before. As the choir set up the sound equipment, he and I talked. He seemed very distant. Even though the bishop had called and "cancelled his cancellation," I sensed the priest was still afraid it might get him in trouble with the bishop! Fortunately the original cancellation had not been given early enough to reach the parishioners. We had an audience of several hundred people.

When time came to begin, I asked the priest, "Will you introduce them or shall I?"

"I don't know them," he said.

I made the introductions. "This is a group of Christian young people from Atlanta, Georgia, USA. They have come to Colombia, at their own expense, to share with you the love and joy they have found in Jesus Christ."

I sat back down beside the priest, who was seated to one side of the choir. As the first few bars of the Colombian national anthem rang out, people rose to their feet. They were deeply moved to hear "gringos" singing "their song." When the anthem ended, thunderous applause broke out. Throughout the rest of the concert the audience sat in rapt attention.

After the anthem ended, I asked the priest, "How did you like that?"

"It was OK," he said with some reservation.

I introduced the second song. When it was over, I said, "That was beautiful, wasn't it?"

"Yes, it was pretty," he answered.

Each successive hymn or anthem melted more ice. When the program ended, the priest stepped to the microphone and gave a glowing, flowery speech about the fine young people who had shared such beautiful music. He exclaimed, "May God bless you as you continue to share the joy you have brought to us tonight!"

Squatters' Shacks and Presidential Palace

During our first 12 years in Colombia, we set up housekeeping in four different rented houses. The last 10 years we lived in a house bought by the Mission. Each time, we selected homes in locations that were neither among the very poor nor the very rich. We wanted to be able to reach down to the needy as well as up to the wealthy. We tried to make our home open to all. Doña María and Don David were among our acquaintances who lived in very poor circumstances.

We also had the opportunity to teach English to some very wealthy women. We gave each an English/Spanish New Testament and used that as our teaching material.

My friendship with Padre García Herreros provided opportunities to share with numerous business, military, and political leaders (including four presidents). Over the years I tried to maintain contact with people in the Presidential Palace.

When the choir from Atlanta sang for the president's wife, we offered to give Spanish New Testaments to all who worked in the Palace. When I asked how many would be needed, the Palace spokesperson said about 650! The number surprised me. Later, I was surprised by the eagerness with which they received the New Testaments.

Another musical incident involved a singing group of Colombians. Missionaries Jim and Kay Harless had organized a small choir of Baptist young people from Barranquilla. The choir sang beautifully. The Colombian Baptist Convention was meeting in Bogotá, and this choir sang several times during the meetings. Leo and Cielo Guzmán, professional singers who had recently come to know the Lord, also sang at the convention.

After one of the sessions, Kay came to me and asked, "Marion, can you get permission for us to serenade the president's wife?"

Her request caught me by surprise. I replied, "I don't know, but we can try."

I knew the secretary to the first lady, so I called her and asked if the two groups could serenade Mrs. Turbay, wife of then president Julio César Turbay Ayala.

The secretary asked, "When did you have in mind?"

"Any night this week that would be convenient with the first lady," I answered. "What about Thursday night at nine o'clock?"

The secretary agreed to check with Mrs. Turbay and told me to call the next day.

When I called the next day, she said, "Mrs. Turbay would be delighted to hear them sing." I took this as a confirmation of the day and hour and shared the news with the two groups.

Just before nine o'clock Thursday night, we drove to the front of the Presidential Palace in a van and a car. I got out and walked toward the heavily guarded iron entrance. One of the guards asked, "May I help you?"

"We are here to serenade the president's wife."

"Serenade?" he asked. "We know nothing of a serenade!"

"I made the arrangements through Mrs. Turbay's secretary the day before yesterday," I answered.

"Just a minute, let me ask the officer in charge."

In a moment the captain of the guard came to the gate and asked, "What is this about a serenade?"

I repeated what I had said to the first guard.

"There must be some mistake," he said. "We have not been given any information about a serenade!"

"Captain, I talked personally with Doña Gladys (the first lady's secretary). She said Mrs. Turbay wanted to hear these people sing!"

He ordered the massive gate be unlocked and invited me inside. The gate locked behind me.

"Come with me!" He ordered and walked across the huge lobby to a telephone.

I gave him my card. "Unless I misunderstood, the serenade

was scheduled for tonight at nine o'clock," I repeated.

He picked up the phone, dialed, talked a moment, then handed the phone to me. It was Mrs. Turbay. "To whom am I speaking?" she asked.

"This is Reverend Marion Corley. I spoke with Doña Gladys earlier this week and understood you were expecting a group to sing for you tonight," I said.

"Yes, she spoke to me about it, but I was expecting a re-confirmation, which never came."

I apologized for the mix up. "The group is here now if you can receive them."

While I talked to her, the captain kept his ear as close as he could to the telephone so he could hear what she was saying to me. I tilted the receiver from my ear so he could hear clearly.

Mrs. Turbay asked to speak with the captain again. I handed him the phone. "Si, Señora! . . . Si, Señora! . . . Si, Señora!" he exclaimed as she spoke. He hung up the phone and said, "The president and his wife have a guest for dinner. They are almost ready to begin the meal. (A late dinner is customary in South American countries.) The serenade will have to be brief. Ask your people to come in."

I walked to the iron gate and motioned for the others to come in. The guards were taken by surprise when the captain ordered them to unlock the gate. The captain said to me, "The group will sing one song, the couple one song, and the group will sing another. That will be all because we don't want to delay the president's dinner."

"That will be fine with us," I answered, relieved that we had received permission.

Two people carried guitar cases and each woman carried a purse. As expected, all had to be thoroughly searched. While the search was being done, the captain asked me, "Where are these people from and who are they?"

"They are Baptist young people from Barranquilla," I answered.

"They are? I'm from Barranquilla," he said.

"That's interesting. Do you know the Clinica Bautista (Baptist Clinic)?" I asked.

"Yes I do! Two of my children were born there. It is a fine hospital!"

I could feel the ice beginning to melt. Before the security search was completed, however, another officer approached the captain. The captain spoke with him briefly, then turned to me, "Because of the delay, the president and his guest have begun their dinner, before it gets cold. The serenade will have to wait until they have finished their dinner."

"That is no problem," I answered. "We are in no hurry."

Actually, this delay worked to our advantage. The guitars had to be tuned, then retuned, because it was a cold night. (Homes in Bogotá are not usually heated.) As the captain chatted with the group, he became more friendly.

Finally, the guards ushered us into a reception hall. Three massive chairs were placed side by side. The captain indicated where the group was to stand. The president, his wife, and their guest, a foreign ambassador, would be seated in front of them. "Since they will have finished dinner, I think the group could sing two songs, the couple two songs, and the group two more songs," the captain said.

"Whatever you say, sir, will be fine with us," I answered. To say I was pleased was an understatement!

After a brief time, the president, his wife, and the visiting ambassador strolled into the room and took their seats. Each group sang as the captain had suggested. After the last song, Mrs. Turbay motioned for the captain and whispered something to him. He came to me and said, "Mrs. Turbay would like for the couple to sing another song. She has enjoyed them very much." They were more than willing to oblige!

When the serenade ended, the three hosts shook hands with the singers and thanked them for an enjoyable evening. That night, the singers didn't walk out of the palace—they floated out!

A Man from the Moon

Astronaut James B. Irwin, who went to the moon in Apollo 15, visited Colombia in July 1972 as guest speaker at an International Baptist Laymen's Conference. When I learned he was coming, I contacted Padre García Herreros to ask if he would like Irwin to give his testimony on the TV program "Minuto de Dios." The priest was pleased with the prospect.

I contacted Irwin by short wave radio to see if he could fit it into his schedule. He would have to come a day earlier than planned, but he was happy to do so. I promised to meet his plane in Bogotá. He was to have his testimony, abbreviated to 3½ minutes, written out. We would have time before the broadcast for me to translate it into Spanish. Jim would speak in English and I would do a simultaneous translation into Spanish. Everything was set—or so we thought!

When the flight from Miami arrived, I waited for Jim and his wife, Mary, to debark. I had never met them, nor seen a picture of them, so to each "gringo" couple I saw, I asked, "Colonel Irwin?" None responded. Several newsmen and photographers also waited to interview or photograph the famous astronaut. When they didn't deplane, the newsmen thought the couple was avoiding them. A flight attendant assured us all passengers had debarked. What had happened?

The program's broadcast was only two hours away, and the guest speaker could not be found! I went to Padre García Herreros and told him Irwin had not been on the flight. "Don't worry," he said, "the young man who is scheduled to speak tomorrow can go on tonight."

"If it is possible to videotape Colonel Irwin's testimony to broadcast at a later date, would you want to do that?"

"Yes, that would be fine," he said.

I was relieved to be off the hook, but I must confess, I was a bit angry at the Lord. "How could You let this happen?" I complained. It was almost a year later before that question was answered.

Jim and Mary arrived on the next flight. He explained, "When we got to Miami, for some reason we didn't have a reservation on the flight to Bogotá, and the flight was full." You would think someone of his fame would not suffer such a fate.

Several events were scheduled for the next day. We went to the Presidential Palace where Irwin presented a small Colombian flag and a microfilm copy of the Bible to the president's chief of staff. The Apollo crew had carried flags of all the nations and the microfilms to the moon. The President said later that these were some of his most treasured mementos. Later that same day Irwin was interviewed by the US Information Service. Irwin thought it would be a radio interview, but when we arrived at the studios he was told it would be a TV interview as well. He said, "I wish I had my photos which were taken on the moon. I left them in the hotel room."

"I'll be glad to go get them while you do the radio interview," I offered.

We were on the 18th floor of a sparsely occupied office building, and only one elevator was in service. I waited for what seemed an eternity. It finally came but it was going up! I thought, I can beat it down by taking the stairs. I started down. When I got to the first floor, the door was locked! I started back up until I found an unlocked door on about the 10th floor. I could do nothing but wait for the elevator. Finally it came. I ran to the hotel, three blocks away, got the pictures, and ran back to the office building. Bogotá's altitude is over 8,000 feet, and that day I could tell the air was "thin," plus there was a lot of pollution in the air. Even after waiting for the slow elevator, which wasn't so slow this time, I was out of breath.

They had finished the radio interview and were ready to begin the TV spot. The pictures helped Jim explain their

moon walk experiences, and that made the elevator/stairs or-
deal worthwhile. When Mary met my wife a few days later she
said, "Your husband is the most harried man I know."

After finishing the interviews, we took a flight to Cali, the
site of the Laymen's Conference. At the check-in counter
Mary wanted to get something out of her suitcase. It happened
to be the same type as mine, and when she closed her case, I
locked it just like I always lock mine. When we arrived in
Cali, Jim and Mary were caught up in a whirlwind of activities.

The next day when we saw one another again, she told
me, "When we got to the hotel last night about midnight, I
started to get ready for bed and discovered my suitcase was
locked. We didn't have a key and had to get the maintenance
man at the hotel to force the lock open with a screwdriver!"
Mary probably still remembers me as "the man who locked my
suitcase in Bogotá!"

Not long after, we returned to the US on furlough. Jim was
scheduled to do some programs for the Baptist Radio and TV
Commission in Fort Worth, Texas, so we made arrangements
with a local TV station to make the videotape for the "Minuto
de Dios" program. Hugo Ruiz, one of the staff at the Commission, was born in Colombia and had served there as pastor of
one of the largest Baptist churches. Spanish was his first language, so he planned to do the Spanish voice-over as Jim
spoke in English. This was what I had planned to do in Bogotá
on live TV. The two tried it several times. Jim's style of speaking in long phrases and technical terms made this a very difficult task, however.

Finally Hugo said, "Colonel Irwin, go ahead and speak in
English. I will do a 'voice-over dubbing' later." When I saw
the problems Hugo and Jim were experiencing, I knew why
the Lord hadn't let him come to Bogotá on that first flight! I
prayed, "Lord, thank You for not letting me make a fool of myself and mess up the program!"

Another advantage to having the testimony on videotape

was that it was later used in several other Spanish speaking countries. Will we ever learn to trust God's wisdom completely?

A Friend in Need

The youth choir of the Lakeside Baptist Church, Dallas, toured Colombia in August 1984. As usual, I met them at the airport in Bogotá to serve as their tour guide. As they were going through customs, the official in charge looked at the two large cases containing their sound equipment. It included large speakers, an amplifier, and an electric keyboard. The official said, "I cannot permit this to enter the country. It is too expensive."

I explained to him that it was for the concert tour and that it would be taken out of the country when the choir left in ten days. I suggested that he register it in the passport of Charles Collins, the choir's director. This would make it necessary to take the equipment out of the country in order for Charles to leave. Still, the man said he could not authorize the equipment's release.

I had heard others tell of similar experiences at customs. A few dollars' bribe would probably have moved things along without delay. However, I didn't feel that was the Christian response.

We loaded the few pieces that had been released onto a waiting truck; the rest was left at the customs office. The choir boarded a bus and we headed for the hotel.

After they were checked in, I told Charles I would see what I could do to obtain the release of the equipment. The expression used for getting such things done in Colombia is "palanca," which literally means a pry pole or leverage. Sometimes it is necessary for someone well known to "put in a good word" to get things moving.

I tried to call my priest-friend García Herreros. He carried a lot of weight in Colombia, and the first concert was to be in the art museum next to his church. The first concert was only hours away. I couldn't reach him by phone, so I took a taxi to his neighborhood. When I arrived, I found that he had finished his lunch and was taking a siesta. I waited almost an hour, but still he had not returned to his office. Time was working against me.

I knew his secretary quite well, so I asked her if it would be OK for me to compose a letter to the customs officials, let her type it, and have it waiting for his signature as soon as he got back to the office. That would save precious time. She agreed, so I dictated the letter to her and she typed it on his official stationery.

The letter appealed for the release of the detained equipment. It told that President Belisario Betancour had been invited to the concert that night, and it mentioned the impact the concerts would have on the people of Colombia. It also stated that Padre García Herreros would personally guarantee that the equipment would be taken out of the country at the time the choir left. I knew I was asking a lot of the priest to assume that responsibility.

When the priest returned to his office, we showed him the letter. He read it, picked up his pen, and signed it without any changes. "Just leave me a copy for my files," he said.

With the letter in hand, I took a taxi to the airport immediately. "Lord, please let this touch the heart of the customs officials!" I prayed on the way. When I got to the airport a different official was in charge. I explained the situation to him. He read the letter and said, "I'm sorry, but I can't help you."

Who had the authority to release the equipment? I asked. He named a certain official in the central office downtown. By this time it was too late to go downtown, get the authorization, return, get the equipment, and take it to the choir in time for the concert. I asked if he would call the central office and ask for the authorization by phone. He said he couldn't do it. "Please, sir," I said, "the president has been invited to the concert tonight. It will be very embarrassing to give the concert without this equipment." He picked up the phone, called the central office, and read the letter. A moment of hesitation followed. The answer apparently was no. The official tried again, "The president will not be happy if the program does not go well." The official on the other end authorized the release! I breathed a deep sigh of relief and said a hearty "thank you!" to the official and to the Lord!

Now, how would I get the equipment to Minuto de Dios? Taxis were readily available, but they were much too small. I called the home of a missionary in Bogotá, Baine Daniels. His wife answered the phone and said, "Baine isn't here. He took some friends who are leaving town to the airport." I asked if the flight was national or international. She said it was national, so I hurried from the international section to the national. I breathed a prayer, "Lord, please help me find him!" I did, in about one minute! Baine was driving a station wagon big enough for the large cases. We quickly loaded the equipment and drove to Baine's home, where he handed me the keys. I hurried to the concert site.

I arrived about ten minutes before concert time. The Colombian Baptist Seminary had loaned the choir its set of handbells. The choir had them set up and were preparing to sing a cappella. They rapidly mounted the sound system and gave their concert without a hitch. The program concluded with "Viva Colombia!," their theme song which I had composed especially for this tour. It was dedicated to President Betancour. He didn't come, but the fact that he had been invited, plus the letter from the priest, had played an important part in getting the equipment released. We later sent a cassette of the concert to the president. We also sent a copy of the sheet music to "Viva Colombia!" printed on gold foil. He sent a very warm letter of appreciation.

The old saying, "A friend in need is a friend indeed" is certainly true. The strong friendship between Padre García Herreros and I played a valuable part in the success of the 13 concerts that were presented in 10 different cities of Colombia.

Closed Door, Open Door

The Lakeside church youth choir had the privilege of singing at the opening session of the Colombian national congress. The opportunity came about in an unusual way. As I was planning the group's itinerary, I wondered if this could be arranged. Accomplishing it would certainly need some "palanca." I remembered that several years before I had met Representative Archibald, from San Andres Islands. Missionary John Thomas, who worked on the island, had introduced us. I went to the capitol building to contact Representative Archibald. The man at the front desk directed me to a suite on the second floor where a number of representatives had their offices. When I arrived, the door to the suite was closed; not even a receptionist was present. It was Friday afternoon, perhaps all had gone home early. How could I contact Representative Archibald, I wondered? I could not return for several days.

The sound of a typewriter came from an open door just a few feet away. I thought, could I leave a note for him? Inside the door, a woman was seated at a desk, hard at work.

"Excuse me," I said, "I hate to bother you, but I need to contact Representative Archibald. His office is closed. If I leave a note, could you get it to him early Monday morning?"

"Yes," the woman answered, "I would be glad to."

She continued to type while I wrote the note on my calling card. The note stated our desire and asked him if he could make the arrangements. When I finished, I handed the card to the woman and asked if it was clearly stated. She read it and said yes. Then she began to read the other information on the card. It gave my name, address, and phone number in Bucaramanga. Below my name was the title "Ambassador of Jesus Christ." Below this was the instruction See Reverse Side. On the reverse side was 2 Corinthians 5:17, 20: "We are ambassadors for Christ, as though God did beseech you by us: we pray you in Christ's stead, be ye reconciled to God. Therefore, if any man be in Christ, he is a new creature: old things are passed away; behold, all things are become new" (KJV).

The woman seemed to contemplate what it said. After a moment, she asked, "Are you related to Angela Corley?"

"She happens to be my daughter," I answered.

"She and my daughter were very good friends at the Panamerican School in Bucaramanga!" the woman responded.

I learned the woman was secretary to a senator who had served as governor for our state, Santander. She said, "I think we may be able to make the necessary arrangements for you."

Some might say, "What a coincidence!" but I think it was more than that. I am convinced it was God's providence. Not only was this woman at work in the right place at the right time, but when I returned a few days later I learned that Representative Archibald had been defeated in the last election! If his office had been open that first day, his secretary would have told me that and I would have had no other contact. You may have heard the expression, "When God shuts a door, He opens a window." This time He opened another door.

When the day came for the choir to sing, I went inside the capitol to receive instructions. The choir had to wait outside, on the front steps. Charles Collins, the choir's director, led it in singing several songs, including "Viva Colombia!" and other Christian songs. They had a large and attentive audience during their wait. Once inside, they sang the Colombian national anthem for the opening session of congress.

I thank God for opening closed doors!

Beginning in Barranca

Our church in Bucaramanga was growing. A Colombian pastor was leading the church well. In addition, the new church in Cúcuta was progressing under the leadership of missionary Jimmy Stiles. This gave me more time to devote to developing work in new areas.

The city God brought to my attention was Barrancabermeja. (That's more than a mouthful even for Colombians, so people there call it Barranca.) Barranca was a 15 minute flight or a three hour drive from Bucaramanga over very rough roads. About the same time, Leopoldo Bowie, a Baptist layman who worked in Barranca, asked us if we could help him start a church there. God's timing was perfect again! I made plans to fly down, get to know the city, and rent a house which could serve as our beginning location.

The most promising building available was an old house which had been used as a restaurant. We would have to do quite a bit of work before it resembled a church. I hired a carpenter/painter to do the work and drew up a contract with him. The work would take several weeks.

During that time, I attended a meeting with pastors and missionaries from all over Colombia, and I asked them to pray for us as we made plans to start this new mission. Our plan was to visit homes during the day, giving out Gospel portions and selling Bibles. At night we would show a film and give a brief sermon. I invited any pastors who could to join us. Two pastors said they could help; the others agreed to support us in prayer. One of those two had much experience selling Bibles door to door. The other said he had relatives living in Barranca who were not Christians. He would stay with them and trust that they would come to know the Lord.

Our oldest son, Bruce, had just finished high school in the US, and was spending two months with us before starting college. The campaign occurred during his visit, and he was a great help. At the time, I was recovering from back surgery, so I flew to Barranca while Bruce drove the two pastors in our jeep.

Unbeknownst to us, a family in Barranca was experiencing a crisis. The son had a large lump growing on his forehead. The doctor could not diagnose it and wanted to operate on him. Naturally, the mother was concerned. The family's maid told the mother, "Don't be worried. God can help your son get well. I will ask our church to pray for him. You need to trust God. He loves you and your son!" Those prayers were answered. The doctor operated and the child recovered. The mother, Ester Rodao, expressed gratitude to God and began attending the maid's church, a pentecostal church.

The Lord was preparing the husband, also. Miguel Rodao worked in the personnel department of a large government oil refinery in Barranca. He had traveled to Bogotá to interview prospective employees for the company and was staying in a "pensión" (a house that had been converted into a small hotel). Another man, who was staying in the same pensión, had made an enemy of a third man. Seeking revenge, the third man threw a can of gasoline into the house, set it afire, and barred the door to prevent escape. Somehow, Miguel escaped alive. This incident made him realize he was not ready to meet God. When he returned home, Ester, his wife, invited him to attend church with her and the children. He began taking them and standing outside and listening, but he didn't like the noisy way they worshiped.

Miguel's parents were from Barranquilla. They lived near a Baptist church, and when he visited them he noticed Baptists were more orderly in their worship. When his wife, Ester, would invite him to go to church he would say, "I would rather go to a Baptist church."

The house I had chosen and prepared for our mission just happened to be located directly across the street from Miguel's home. He told me later that as the contractor began painting

98

a sign on the front of the building, he watched as it spelled out, in Spanish, "BAPTIST CHURCH. God is Love." He could hardly believe his eyes! He called to Ester and said, "We will have to go there!"

Another sign of God's work was in store for us. Remember that one of the pastors who came to help had said, "I have relatives in Barranca." Those relatives happened to be the Rodaos.

Miguel, Ester, and their children began attending every service of the new church. They were like sponges, soaking up everything they heard from the films and the preaching. Soon both husband and wife accepted Christ as Saviour. They were the first people I baptized in Barranca. By nature Miguel was rather shy and timid, and it was thrilling to see him grow in his faith. He had an old pickup truck which he used to bring people to church. He would carry so many in it, sometimes I thought his tires would explode. Little by little he grew more courageous. Eventually he became a teacher and even preached at times when the church had no pastor.

Building in Barranca

The Lord blessed our efforts in Barranca, and we witnessed a slow growth in believers. They grew in numbers as well as maturity and began serving as teachers and leaders. One young man I had baptized in Bucaramanga, Roberto, quit his job in another city to come to Barranca. He found a part-time job there and served as caretaker and lay preacher of the church. I tried to visit Barranca almost every weekend, but when I couldn't be there, Roberto taught Sunday School and preached. Little by little Miguel began doing these jobs, also. In addition, Leopoldo, who had originally asked me to start the church, helped, but he often had to work on Sundays.

As the congregation grew we identified two needs: a Colombian pastor for the church and a larger, permanent place of worship. The Lord sent us a pastor, Carlos Puerta, who had been studying at the Baptist seminary in Cali. He was a hard worker, and with his leadership, the church continued to grow. We requested funds from the Lottie Moon Christmas Offering to buy property and build the sanctuary and some classroom space. We were granted $25,000 to do so. Finding some property was not as dramatic as in Bucaramanga, but we were able to find adequate property at a reasonable price. The property was a vacant lot about 65 feet wide and 175 feet deep.

One day Miguel came to me and said, "Don Mario, the refinery where I work has some discarded steel rafters that I think we might could use to build the roof of the new church."

"Would they sell them or donate them?" I asked.

"I think they will give them to us. If not, I'm sure they wouldn't charge much. If you would like, I will make a formal request." In about three weeks we had our answer. It was yes, and they even delivered them to the building site! The rafters were from some of the original construction when North

Americans had built the refinery. They were made of *double* 3½ inch angle, which was much stronger than today's rafters of this size, and they were 38 feet long. There were seven, as I remember, five the same size and two slightly longer. We cut one of the longer ones down to match the five and saved the other for future use. This was the first time I had ever designed a building to fit the rafters, rather than the rafters to fit the building! The building plans were drawn and approved, and we began digging the foundation.

As we progressed, Miguel told me he had also found some long steel beams at the refinery which could serve to reach from rafter to rafter to hold up the roofing. He said he had put in a request for them, also. That would help us save money, and we could build more than we originally thought we could.

The concrete and steel columns were built. The refinery even sent a heavy duty crane to put the rafters in place. The rafters were so strong they were much too heavy to put in place with the primitive building method used in Bucaramanga. We would soon need the steel beams or we would have to come up with an alternative plan. I asked Miguel if he had received an answer to his request. He said he had asked several times but the response was always, "We haven't heard anything from the main office in Bogotá."

I was scheduled to go to Bogotá the following week. I asked, "Don Miguel, do you think it would do any harm if I went by the main office and checked on the status of the request?"

"No," he answered. "I've done all I can do from here. Give it a try."

I had met the president of the company on a previous occasion. He was from Bucaramanga and had been instrumental in starting the Panamerican School, where our children studied.

I made an appointment with him. Upon arrival, I was ushered into the most impressive executive office I had ever seen. We chatted a few moments and I thanked him for the donation of the rafters and the crane to lift them in place. I mentioned Miguel, whom he knew very well. "Miguel is a member of our church," I said. "Several other refinery workers either are members or attend the church. I am convinced that when a man comes to know the Lord, he is a better person in every way, including the work that he does." I told him about the request for the beams and asked if he knew if the request would be granted.

He replied, "I don't know about it. I will ask my assistant to look into it." He rang for him, and in just a moment the assistant came in. The president introduced us and said, "Reverend Corley is building a Baptist church in Barranca. They are supplying us with some good workers. They have made a request for some materials. See what you can do to move it along."

The assistant showed me into an adjoining office. We sat down facing each other across a huge executive desk. He said, "You say this is for a Baptist church in Barranca?"

"Yes sir, it is."

"I'm Roman Catholic," he said.

I thought to myself, well you have put your foot in your mouth now, Marion!

"But," he continued, "when I was in the US working on my graduate degree, a Baptist church helped me, and especially my wife, in so many ways that I will do all that I can to help you get what you need."

In about ten days the beams were delivered to the construction site.

This experience taught me the importance of ministering to foreign students in America. American churches can sow seed in the hearts of people who, when they return to their own countries, will be in influential places of leadership. Remember what 1 Corinthians 15:58 says, "Be ye stedfast, unmoveable, always abounding in the work of the Lord, forasmuch as ye know that your labour is not in vain in the Lord" (KJV).

Over time, this assistant and I became good friends. He invited me to his home to share a meal with his family. Before we began dinner, he said, "Mario, we have a custom of joining hands and praying before we eat. Please join us." I have an idea they learned that action from the American Christians who had ministered to them in so many ways.

A beam is raised into place at the construction site of the church in Barranca.

Angels Watching Over Me

Have you ever seen an angel? Do you even believe in them?

I have never seen an angel—at least that I recognized as such. However, they have done more for you and me than we will ever know, this side of heaven. A special verse to me is Psalm 34:7, "The angel of the Lord encampeth round about them that fear him, and delivereth them" (KJV).

The following are events where I know God protected me, perhaps through an angel. The kind young man in the story "Get the Gringo!" may have been one. I had never seen a student on strike who was that kind!

When we were constructing the roof of the church in Barranca, the beams were difficult to position. They were more than 20 feet long and weighed more than 200 pounds each. To lift them from the ground to the top of the rafters we had to use two "block and tackles." These are multiple pulleys and ropes that make it easier to lift heavy objects. It took nine men to place a beam: three on one block and tackle, three on the other block and tackle, and three on the rafters to receive the beam, put it in its proper place, and bolt it down.

The men on the block and tackle teams would raise a beam about ten feet in the air. One team would stop pulling, while the other continued to pull until one end of the beam was within reach of the team on top. Once the end of the beam was resting on a rafter, the first block and tackle had to be disconnected; then the other team would raise their end as the men on top worked it over the adjoining rafter. It was a slow and crude process, but it worked.

The two block and tackles and ropes we were using were borrowed and appeared to be in good shape. I was a member of the team on top. The beam was raised to the first position and the first team stopped pulling. The second team continued to pull. All appeared well, and the first block and tackle was disconnected. The second team had their end almost to the top when, to my horror, the rope began to break! I called out to the men, "Stop! The rope is breaking!"

Of the three strands, two were broken and the third was slowly unwinding and about to snap! It would have been a major tragedy had that happened. The man on the very top of the rafter was holding the end of the beam under his arm. If the rope had broken, the beam would have thrown him like a catapult. Who knows what would have happened to the rest of us?

The three of us standing on top held on for dear life. We were in too difficult a position to raise that much weight. The block and tackle team could only hold their rope still, because when they tried to raise the beam, the rope continued to unwind. There was some heavy, silent praying going on! We finally wrestled it into place and breathed a sigh of relief. I invited the men and the three women who were preparing our lunch to join me as I thanked God for helping us do what had humanly seemed impossible. The next thing I did was buy new rope for the block and tackles. Fortunately, we had no more problems with the rest of the beams.

Several weeks later while in Bogotá visiting another missionary, I told him about the experience and said, "I still don't know how we got that beam in place without it falling."

He replied, "Marion, if you had looked around, you might have seen a ruptured angel."

I doubt that angels suffer injury, but I do know God surely gave us help from some source. Again I said, "Thank You, Father!"

All Alone?

Is a Christian ever alone? Not if we let the Lord walk with us! At times we may feel alone, but Jesus promised to send the Holy Spirit to be with us. "And I will ask the Father, and He will give you another Helper, that He may be with you forever" (John 14:16 NASB).

My work made it necessary for me to be away from home often. Evelyn and the children adapted well to my absences, and we relied on the Lord's promises to keep us safe.

One day only Evelyn and Angela were at home. Evelyn had to leave for a short while, and after she left, Angela, about 12-years-old at the time, locked the front door and put the safety chain in its locked position.

Not long after Evelyn drove off, the door bell rang. Angela looked out the window to see a man standing at the front gate. Through the open window she asked him, "May I help you?"

The man asked for me by name and mentioned a receipt for some money he had paid me. She could not hear him well, so she moved to the front door, made sure the chain was in place, and opened the door enough to be able to understand him. She then noticed that as she moved to the door he had moved from the gate to the door.

"I paid your father some money and he was to leave a receipt for me," he repeated.

"I'm sorry, but I don't know anything about it," she answered.

At that moment the man noticed there was slack in the chain; he reached inside and unhooked the chain.

The man came in, repeated what he had said about a receipt, and said, "I'll just wait for him." A moment later he said, "I think I'll look around and see if I can find it." He went into my office, looked around, then went upstairs. Angela stayed behind him every step. In her innocence she was more

106

concerned that a stranger was in her house than the fact she could be in grave danger.

He entered the guest room, picked up a few articles, smelled them, and put them down. Next, he went into my and Evelyn's bedroom and looked through every drawer. He found some pesos we had on hand, handed them to Angela, and said, "You take these. I don't want somebody to think I'm a thief!" He found Evelyn's jewelry, looked at it, and put it back.

He went into Angela's room but left when he saw it was a little girl's room. Next, he stepped across the hall into Bryan's room and went through it closely. He sniffed each item he picked up. He smelled the sheets on the bed, books, clothes— everything. He mumbled something about not finding the receipt and left the room.

In her innocence, Angela tried to straighten up things in Bryan's room. That gave him just enough time to return to my and Evelyn's room and get the money Angela had put back in the drawer. He also took some of Evelyn's jewelry. It wasn't worth much money, but it had sentimental value to her.

The man met Angela as she left Bryan's room and said, "I guess I'll have to come back later for the receipt." With that he left.

Angela locked the door behind him. She wondered why the man had acted so strange. When Evelyn returned, Angela began telling her what had happened. She giggled some as she talked.

Evelyn asked her, "Did the man touch you or bother you in any way?"

"No, he just went through the house looking and sniffing," Angela answered.

Evelyn looked in her jewelry drawer and the drawer where the money had been. Both were missing. She called a member of our church and told him what had happened. The member called the police, who came and wrote out a report. Angela gave a good description of the thief.

The police said, "We think he is the same man we have received similar complaints about. He was probably looking for drugs. If you see him again, please call us."

When I arrived home two days later, Angela told me about the incident. She still had a nervous giggle as she talked. After making sure he had not harmed her, I checked the chain on the front door. It had not been mounted properly, and the extra slack had allowed enough room for the man to reach in and unhook it. It took me about three minutes to correct that!

As I worked on the chain, anger began boiling up inside me. You dirty rat! I wish I could get my hands on you! I thought vindictively. As I reflected further, however, my anger turned to gratitude. "Thank You, Father, for being here to protect my daughter!" I gratefully prayed. We lost less than $200, but Angela could have been raped or killed. Angels were watching over my "angel."

Growing in Grace

I am always thrilled to see persons come to know the Lord. The Word of God begins to take root in their hearts, and He begins to change them as they grow in grace.

Eduardo Sánchez was a poor, uneducated, crude man who sometimes drank heavily and became cruel and abusive to his wife and family. After one such episode of drinking and violence, his wife ran him off. He was living alone and was very unhappy. One night while listening to a religious radio program, the Bible message touched his heart and made him feel his need for God. At the end of the message the preacher invited listeners to open their hearts and let God enter their lives, ask for His forgiveness, and begin a new life in Christ. Eduardo knelt beside his bed and asked Jesus into his heart.

The Lord began to change Eduardo. He stopped drinking and returned to his wife and family. He told them what had happened to him and asked their forgiveness for his past actions.

During this time, Rosa, his wife, was working in the home of a Christian family. The woman of the house shared the good news with her, and she gave her heart to Christ.

Eduardo and Rosa and their two children began attending our church regularly. It was beautiful to see the transformation taking place in their lives and home. The Bible replaced the bottle. Love, joy, and peace, fruits of the Spirit, replaced the hatred, bitterness, and bickering. The Bible says, "Therefore if any man be in Christ, he is a new creature: old things are passed away; behold, all things are become new" (2 Cor. 5:17 KJV). We were seeing this very thing happen!

Before Eduardo accepted Christ, he had earned his living selling "ponche." *Ponche* is the Spanish word for punch, but it is more than punch as we know it. This punch was a mixture of fruit, sugar, and water which had been allowed to ferment.

Eduardo made this drink in his home and sold it on the streets from a small wooden pushcart. The cart had a square metal tank which held about five gallons of the drink. A large chunk of ice was added to make it cold. The cart also had a wooden rack which held several glasses and two smaller tanks for washing and rinsing the glasses. After a customer drank all he wanted, the glass was dipped in the "wash" tank, then in the "rinse" tank, and returned to the rack, ready for the next customer. As you can imagine, this was not a very sanitary setup, especially as the day wore on. Perhaps customers felt there was enough alcohol content in the ponche to kill the germs. If not, after a couple of glasses of ponche, who worried about germs?

As Eduardo began to grow in his new-found faith, he decided that selling this drink, even though its alcohol content was low, was not pleasing to the Lord. It was unlikely that anyone drank enough to get drunk. However, some customers "made it through the day" on this drink and then turned to something stronger in the evening. Eduardo did not want to take part in destroying someone's home, as had almost happened to his.

Eduardo was quite poor, so he needed to utilize the same cart, if possible, to start a new business. He thought up a plan to sell snow cones from the cart. With a few changes, the glass rack now held bottles of sweetened, flavored syrup to pour over shaved ice. The largest tank held blocks of ice, and, since the two tanks for washing glasses were no longer needed, a hand-cranked machine mounted in that area shaved the ice.

Eduardo's clientele changed, too. Rather than men at construction sites, his customers were mostly children, going to or from school or playing in the streets. As he prepared the snow cones he talked to the children about God's love, asked them if they went to church, and told them about the change God had made in his life and home.

Eduardo, like Doña María, never had the opportunity to go to school. He wanted very much to learn to read so he could read the Bible. Using a special course designed to teach adults to read, Evelyn helped him learn. What a joy it was for both of them when he began recognizing, first, alphabet letters, then words, and then was able to read a sentence and understand it!

Eduardo felt such gratitude to the Lord for his new life that when he learned about tithing, he said, "I want to give back to the Lord one-tenth of all He helps me earn." Each Sunday he came to church with his offering envelope bulging with coins. Rosa sold slices of fresh fruit and hand-squeezed orange juice from a street corner stand. She found the same joy in giving to the Lord as he had found. Both were a source of inspiration to all of us. Their combined giving could not pay for much, but it had real value to them, to us, and, most of all, to the Lord.

A Brother in Jail

As you can imagine, Eduardo did not make a lot of money selling snow cones. To feed seven family members, it became necessary for him to take a second job. He worked as a night watchman in a small auto repair shop. On several occasions thieves had attempted to enter the building by climbing the high walls or removing some of the roof.

The owner of the shop provided Eduardo with a shotgun to protect the property. Late one night Eduardo heard noises at the front of the shop, so he went to investigate. The sounds were coming from the office area. He turned on the lights and saw that the front door had been broken down. The office door had been forced open, also. A thief had taken some tools and was returning for the office equipment. When Eduardo turned on the lights, he thought the thieves, upon seeing him, would run. This was not the case, however.

One man began advancing toward him in a threatening manner. Eduardo knew his life was in danger. He raised the shotgun to fire a warning shot. The blast hit the thief, however. The thief turned away, went out the front door, and collapsed on the sidewalk in a pool of blood.

Eduardo called the police. After questioning him, they took him to the police station to file a complete report. They ordered him to report to them every two days until the day of the hearing. Then word came that the thief had died, and this changed everything. Eduardo was put in jail. Colombian law specified he had to stay there until a judge decided if he would be charged with a crime. In Eduardo's financial condition he could not even think of hiring a lawyer. The state would furnish him one, but most likely it would not be a very capable one. It was common in cases like this that a man was held for months, or even years, before the case came to trial.

When prisoners in the jail learned what had happened and

who had died, some said to Eduardo, "The man you killed was our friend and we will get you for it!" Other prisoners came to his defense. He began to tell any who would listen about the Lord and to pray with them.

When I heard about Eduardo's situation, I called the jail to see if I could visit him. The guard told me he could have no visitors. Then I asked if I could send him a New Testament. He said that I could.

When I arrived at the jail, I went directly to the main desk. There I encountered Gerardo Gutiérrez, the first Colombian I became acquainted with 20 years before.

"Gerardo, what are you doing here?" I asked in surprise.

"I am the assistant director," he answered, equally surprised to see me.

I explained my purpose in being there and asked if I could visit Eduardo.

Gerardo replied, "I'm sorry, Mario. He is being held incommunicado (no visitors), but I will take the Bible to him."

As you can imagine, when church members heard about Eduardo's plight, they became concerned. They began praying earnestly that he would be safe, that the threats against his life would not be carried out, and that he would soon be released. The following Wednesday night, at prayer meeting, we reminded members of his situation and encouraged them to support him in prayer.

About the middle of the service I heard a commotion in the back of the room. I looked to see what had happened. Eduardo had just walked in! We could hardly believe our eyes. The Lord had answered our prayers while we were still praying. I now understand how the early Christians felt when, in the book of Acts, as they prayed for Peter's release he walked into their presence.

Please Help Me Build My House

Eduardo and his family lived in a small lean-to structure. It was all they could afford, although he dreamed of owning his own home one day, no matter how humble. He borrowed some money from the owner of the auto repair shop where he worked to purchase some property, and he paid it back little by little. The property he bought with the loan was not very desirable. It was located outside the city on a hillside. Ironically, the name of this area was El Paraíso (Paradise)! It had no sewer system, no electricity, and no city water lines. The "road" that led to it was little more than a rough, unpaved trail.

The lot was small, about 30-by-30 feet. It sloped from back to front at a 40 degree angle. The slope would make it difficult to build on. Why did Eduardo buy this lot? It was all he could afford.

Even before the loan was paid off he began work on the lot. He built a six foot retaining wall on the front boundary next to the road and dug out the back part of the lot making it more or less level. As you can imagine, this work was back breaking. And it was done all by hand!

One day Eduardo asked me if I would loan him some money. "I have started building my house and I would like for you to see it."

Fortunately, I had a four-wheel drive vehicle. I was saddened by the limits of space and the terrain he had to work with. At the same time, I admired his determination, drive, and dream.

Eduardo had no plans other than the ideas in his head. He told me what he had in mind. From my experience in construction I was able to make some suggestions. "How much money do you want to borrow, Eduardo?" I asked. I don't remember the amount in pesos, but it was about $400. Can you

Eduardo Sánchez's home under construction. Its three small rooms housed seven family members; a large adjoining room later served as a place of worship.

imagine trying to build a house for that?

He had only a few bricks on hand and some second hand roofing. "I want to build three rooms across the front and add to it as I can. I also want to build a large room adjoining them, so we can have a place to start a church," he told me.

"Eduardo, I will be glad to loan you the money," I answered. I knew it would be a long time before he could pay it back—if ever. But he wanted the people to hear the good news that had transformed his life. I did, too.

Eduardo's family consisted of his wife, a teenage daughter, and a son about ten. In addition, his wife's mother, his mother, and his brother lived with them. The brother, about 20-years-old, had contracted polio as an infant. He was about the size of a two-year-old and was confined to a rustic homemade crib/bed because he was completely helpless. All would live in three rooms.

When the house was far enough along for them to "have a roof over their heads," the Sánchez family moved in. Eduardo invited church members to a service of dedication for it. I was not in Colombia at the time, but members sent me a picture of the 39 people who came. They met in the open air, behind the house, but they didn't mind. They rejoiced that Eduardo now had a home of his own.

Don't Let Me Be a Burden

Doña María served people all her life. Raising as many children as she did required that. After she became a Christian, helping others became the joy of her life. She would do anything within her power for anybody. She served others, but she didn't want others to serve her.

Parents usually expect children to see that they are well cared for in old age. That was *not* the case with Doña María, however. She bore a total of 13 children. Several died as infants, others died as young children; only four lived to adulthood. We came to know two of them, a daughter and a son. The other two lived far away. One of those was wealthy, but made no effort to maintain contact nor help her in any way. Her daughter was away most of the time. She would breeze into town for a few days every so often, then disappear like a ghost. More than a year after Doña María had died the daughter called our home, "to see how Mama is!"

Her son Antonio was the most considerate of the four. For a while Doña María lived with him and his common-law wife, but the wife would throw her out whenever she had a disagreement with Doña María.

In these circumstances, it was no surprise that Doña María felt she had no one to care for her. Several times she said to me, "I pray that God will not let me get old and helpless. I don't want to be a burden to anyone."

Doña María had high blood pressure, but she seldom complained. One Saturday while she was staying with us, Doña María told Evelyn that her head was hurting. Evelyn knew the pain *must* be bad for Doña María to complain, so she took her to a hospital emergency room. Doctors gave her some medicine and sent her home.

The next morning Evelyn, Bryan, Angela, and I went to Sunday School and church while Doña María stayed home. A

Doña María, about a year before her death, proudly puts on a sweater given to her by Evelyn Corley.

few minutes after we left a man rang the door bell. She looked out the window, rather than opening the door. The man asked, "Is Don Mario here?"

She answered no.

He said, "He told me to come by at 9:30 to pick up some money he owes me."

"Then why have you come at 9:40?" She asked.

Her answer surprised the man and he left. She was 80-years-old, her head was splitting with pain, yet she still re-

117

membered how to deal with a con artist!

By Sunday afternoon her headache was worse. Evelyn took her back to the hospital. Doctors examined her again, gave her a different prescription, and sent her home. I left to find a drugstore open on Sunday. When I returned, Evelyn said, "Doña María is asleep and I can't wake her."

I could not get her to respond, either. She had a strange look on her face. I said to Evelyn, "Honey, I think we'd better get her to the hospital!"

That was no easy task. Doña María weighed about 180 pounds. With her unconscious, it was like trying to pick up a huge sack of grain. Her cot was wider than the door, so Bryan and I picked up each end of the mattress, carried her through the door and down a narrow passageway, and then pulled the mattress across the floor and out the front door. A neighbor helped us lift her, mattress and all, into our van. This time the hospital kept her, but they offered little encouragement.

I tried to locate Antonio. I couldn't find him, so I left word with a friend. Late that night he called me and we went to the hospital. We could tell that Doña María was dying.

About 4:00 A.M. she died. We contacted several radio stations and asked them to announce her death and scheduled burial. We hoped her daughter would hear, but she didn't.

Doña María was buried the following day in a simple ceremony. Antonio was the only one of her children present. However, a host of her spiritual family was present to celebrate her going home.

Her prayer had been, "God, please don't let me get old and helpless and be a burden to anyone." God answered her prayer.

Why Did We Go?

Many people don't understand why missionaries move their families to foreign lands, far from family and friends, to live and work. It is not for the glamour of travel to faraway places. That wears off fast.

It is not for money. Missionaries' needs are taken care of, but they do not become wealthy on their salaries. A person has the opportunity to earn much more staying in the US. Persons who work for business firms overseas can expect a healthy bonus, especially if they become bilingual.

It is not because missionary life is easy or that everybody will welcome you with open arms.

It is not to earn "points" with God or to earn salvation. God *gives* us eternal life, not because we earn or deserve it, but because of His grace and love.

Missionaries go because God leads them to go. If that is not true, they don't last long!

At the time we were appointed missionaries several church members and friends asked, "Why?" Several even asked, "Are you going to take your children over there?"

To answer their questions as well as my own, I wrote this poem and later set it to music:

The Mission Call

God calls us to a distant land.
We do not go for wealth or fame.
We go that those who have never heard
Might come to trust in His wonderful name.

We leave our home and friends behind.
The cost is high, but not too much.
Remember what our Saviour left

That we might know His heavenly touch?

Chorus

"The fields are white, the laborers are few.
As the Father sent me so send I you."
Go tell all mankind that life can be new
And remember this promise,
"Lo, I am always with you."

Kurt Kaiser wrote a beautiful, simple chorus that has been sung across our land and around the world:

Oh How He Loves You and Me[1]

Oh, how He loves you and me!
Oh, how He loves you and me!
He gave His life, what more could He give?
Oh, how He loves you!
Oh, how He loves me!
Oh, how He loves you and me!

With Kurt's permission, I have added another stanza:

Oh, how I love You, my Lord!
Oh, how I love You, my Lord!
You gave your life, now I give mine to You.
Oh, how I love You!
Oh, how I love You!
Oh, how I love You, my Lord!

It is not enough to bask in the sunlight of His love. The same One who loves us has left us a command that He expects us to carry out. It is, "Go ye therefore . . . unto the end of the world" (Matt. 28:19-20 KJV).

This worldwide task is not just for foreign missionaries. If you are a believer in Jesus Christ, you must find God's will for your life and do it faithfully.

I see three steps we must follow in carrying out the Great Commission. They are like links in a chain, and each must be strong.

Praying

Jesus said in Luke 10:2, "The harvest truly is great, but the labourers are few: pray ye therefore the Lord of the harvest, that he would send forth labourers into his harvest" (KJV). A simple "God, bless the missionaries" is a start, but don't stop there. Learn about missionaries and their work. Take time to discover their prayer requests. Become acquainted with missionaries through letters or their visits to your church.

Giving

Jesus told about a woman who gave a "widow's mite." He said she gave more than the rich who gave out of their abundance. If you do not have much money, like Doña María, God will consider your "widow's mite" a great contribution. Unfortunately, many who give a "mite" are not widows!

Many with plenty
Are giving a "mite."
When we are stingy
That is not right!

Souls that are dying
Can be made alive.
Part of the secret is
Christians must tithe.

Worldwide, Christians give only 2 percent of their income to Christian causes. Only 1 percent of that 2 percent goes to global foreign missions work. Churches must become sacrificial in their giving, also. The world will never be reached for

Christ when more than 90 percent of our resources (financial and human) are used for local needs.

Going

In Isaiah 6, Isaiah records for us a personal encounter with God. The key points of that encounter include:

1. He "saw the Lord, high and lifted up" (v. 1).
2. He saw how sinful and unclean he was before a holy God (v. 5).
3. He found forgiveness and cleansing from God (vv. 6-7).
4. He "heard the voice of the Lord, saying, 'Whom shall I send, and who will go for us?'" (v. 8).
5. He responded, "here am I; send me" (v. 8) (author's paraphrase).

Jesus called average men, with little or no education, then transformed them through His Word and love. He sent them out to "turn the world right-side-up!" Would you like to become like them? In 1987, 250,400 foreign missionaries worked worldwide. Yet there were approximately 425,000 professional ministers in the US alone. In the quietness of your heart, before God, walk the five steps that Isaiah did. God may send you across the street or across an ocean, but He promises to go with you. So do not fear offering yourself to Him!

Could it be there are Christians afraid to say, "Here am I; send me"? Have you, like Paul, answered, "Lord, what will thou have me to do?" (Acts 9:6 KJV).

Dear friend, millions of other Doña Marías live in this world thirsting for the Living Water and hungry for the Bread of Life. May God bless you as you seek His will in bringing them to the feet of Him whose "free gift . . . is eternal life" (Rom. 6:23b NASB).

Leaving Home or Going Home

In January 1985 we had to return to the US on medical leave, which eventually led to medical retirement for me. Were we "leaving home" or "going home"? Actually it was both. In one sense, we were going home, because Evelyn and I were born in the US. Most of our family and many friends lived there.

But we were also leaving home. Bryan and Angela were both born in Bucaramanga. Evelyn and I had lived there more than one-third of our lives and two-thirds of our married life. We had to pull up roots in Colombia 22 years deep among friends, neighbors, and fellow Christians. Most of our Christian brothers and sisters were first generation believers. They would have to assume leadership responsibilities prematurely. Of the four churches and several missions we worked with, only two had Colombian pastors, and both of them went to other churches not long after we left.

It broke our hearts to have to leave with no one to take our places. God knew we were leaving early. Had He not called someone? Or He had called and those He called had not answered?

Those 22 years in Colombia had taken their toll on us. I had undergone back surgery and contracted malaria, typhoid fever, dengue fever, and numerous bouts of intestinal parasites. However, the major factor that had led to my broken health and early retirement was lack of help. We were trying to do the work of three or four couples. We prayed that God would call more persons to help, but those He called did not answer.

Some people have said to us, "You did more than your share." "You should have quit while you were healthy." "No one should suffer as much as you did." I am glad that Jesus never gave in to feelings like that! My answer to them is found in Romans 8:18, "For I consider that the sufferings of this present time are not worthy to be compared with the glory that is to be revealed to us" (NASB).

In Spanish you can say goodbye two ways: "adiós" and "hasta luego." The first phrase means we may not see each other again. The second means, "I will see you later." When it became apparent we would have to leave, I wrote a letter to our friends in Colombia. It was titled, "Adiós or Hasta Luego?" In it, I explained why we were leaving and expressed the hope we would see them in heaven—not because of what we, or they, had done, but because of genuine faith in Jesus Christ and what He had done for us.

Our flight to the US left Colombia at 7:00 A.M., January 16, 1985. When we arrived at the airport we were surprised and thrilled to see a bus load of Christian brothers and sisters from Bucaramanga. They had rented a bus for the occasion so they could see us off.

We shed many tears and expressed Christian love to one another. Then we said, "Hasta luego," wondering, would we see each other again this side of heaven?

His Truth Is Marching On

In July 1988 the First Baptist Church of Bucaramanga celebrated its twentieth anniversary. Members invited Evelyn and me to join them in their celebration. Evelyn could not take any time from her job, so I accepted the invitation, anxious to see my many brothers, sisters, and friends and enjoy three-and-a-half weeks back home in my "second country."

What a time of rejoicing we experienced during this week of special celebration and revival. The former pastors had been invited, also, and we took turns preaching in the church and her missions. Two Baptist missionary couples now lived in Bucaramanga: Larry and Linda Booth appointed by the Foreign Mission Board, SBC, and Idelfonso and Miriam DoSantos appointed by the Brazilian Baptist Convention. Both couples were helping the church reach out to new areas.

The DoSantos family had begun a mission in their home in an upper-class section of the city. This house mission was only a block away from a small drug store operated by Gerardo Gutiérrez and his wife, Dora. You will remember that Gerardo was the first person we met when we arrived in Bucaramanga 25 years before. I was saddened to learn of the death, during our absence, of their lovely teenage daughter. I was able to share with them some Scriptures which brought comfort to their hurting hearts. The last I heard, they were attending the mission services in the DoSantos' home.

Larry and Idelfonso were working together to begin another mission in the town of San Gil. (Remember the short cut with the gas tank on top of the car?) Larry and Idelfonso usually drove to San Gil each Thursday morning, visited during the afternoon, and directed a worship/preaching/training service that night. They returned to Bucaramanga the next day. Through the years I had wanted to start a mission there but was already overextended with the four areas we were

125

working in. I was able to accompany them one Thursday, and it was a joy to preach in this little mission after praying so many years for an opportunity to establish a Baptist witness there. The day I visited, a young woman who had found the Lord about 15 years before in Bucaramanga was also visiting. Rosalba was the first in her family to become a Christian. She now lived in Venezuela, but had planned her vacation so she could attend the anniversary celebrations. Rosalba was originally from San Gil and had returned to witness to and encourage relatives there. I asked her, "Rosalba, how many in your family have come to know the Lord since you accepted Him?" She named 27 relatives! Then she said to others standing nearby, "I hope very soon you, too, will come to know the joy and peace Christ has given me!"

I hoped to visit the church in Barranca, also. When I mentioned this to Larry, however, he said, "Marion, don't even *think* of going to Barranca! The US Embassy has declared it an unsafe area." When I read the newspapers I understood why. On several occasions assassinations had occurred in and around Barranca. One day five persons were killed. Another weekend, the military discovered a plot by terrorists named "a weekend of tears." Terrorists had planned widespread acts of terrorism to create confusion and fear.

Why would they want to do that? you wonder. Terrorists want to disrupt progress and undermine peace in Colombia. Barranca, home to the largest oil refinery in the country, is essential to the normal functioning of the country. That makes it a prime target for terrorism.

Instead of visiting Barranca, a few of the church members came to Bucaramanga, and I was able to visit with them there.

During the week of revival I anxiously awaited my turn to preach in El Paraíso, where Eduardo Sánchez and his family lived. You may remember his goal was to add a large room onto his three room house in order to start a mission. I rejoiced to see he had accomplished his goal. Not only that, he had made deposits, little by little, to the treasurer of the church and had managed to pay back the pesos I had loaned him! The pesos had only about one-third their buying power now because of inflation, but the important part was he had not forgotten his promise.

When we arrived for the service that night, Eduardo proudly showed me his home. He had also built a roof over most of the remaining lot, and the mission had been meeting there. Even so, the people who attended could not fit into this space! We held the service in the street in front of his house. More than a hundred people stood listening to the singing and preaching. It thrilled me to see what this poor, simple, uneducated but dedicated man had accomplished for the Lord. How I wish every follower of our Lord would be this faithful. I was also happy to learn that the Bucaramanga church had helped buy a lot just up the street so that this congregation could have a separate building. I donated the pesos Eduardo had paid back to help pay construction costs.

My visit to Colombia was all too short. I did get to see many old friends, however. Leonor, the student we met in Alabama, now lives in England. She happened to be in Bucaramanga the same time I was, and I had a good visit with her and her aged mother.

My last stop in Colombia was in Bogotá for a brief visit with my friend, Padre García Herreros. He was not well. His age had caused him to slow down considerably, but younger priests, with his same goals and vision, were carrying on his dreams of bringing the people to a personal faith and commitment to Jesus Christ.

1992 Update

January 1992 the Colombian Baptist Convention celebrated its fiftieth anniversary. They invited retired missionaries to join them for this special occasion. Evelyn and I accepted their invitation. It was a joyful time as we joined with Christian brothers and sisters we had not seen for many years. We were given a special plaque marking this historic occasion. Most of the older missionaries were gone by then, but we met many of the new ones, though their number is smaller.

We rejoiced to see a number of people whom we had played a part in their coming to know the Lord, and who are now in positions of leadership in the Convention and/or in their local churches.

After the Convention celebration ended, we visited friends in Bogotá, Bucaramanga, and Cúcuta. In Bogotá we saw various Baptist friends. We also went to see our priest-friend-brother García Herreros. He was to celebrate his eighty-third birthday the following day. He is in better health now than when I visited in 1988, but he has turned most of his duties over to others who are younger but who share his vision and goals. Behind his church, friends have created a small jungle garden. It shuts out the noise and creates a quietness that is very peaceful. We found our brother in his small study surrounded by some of his favorite books and his Bible. Also, in this garden is a small prayer chapel where we joined our hearts before the Lord in prayer.

In Bucaramanga we enjoyed visits with a number of brothers and friends (some came from Barranca, also), who remained from our 22 years of missions work. Remember Gerardo Gutiérrez, the first person we came to know in Bucaramanga? He and his wife, Dora, came to our hotel, and we shared many memories. The most beautiful part was when they told us that each of them had accepted Christ as personal

Lord and Saviour. "We are not worried about material things now, nor are we afraid of dying!" they said. Then they added, "Why did we wait so long? Why did we waste all those years?" The seed we had sown had sprouted and grown. They are not Baptists but are busy sharing their faith in "house churches."

We were able to see Eduardo Sánchez, also. On Sunday afternoon we went to El Paraíso, to the mission that was started in his home.

We were glad to see that there is now water, lights, sewage, and natural gas, and parts of the street are paved. (Each property owner gets his part paved when he has the money.) However, the greatest thrill for us was to see that the small property purchased for the mission is now usable. The first floor (or basement) serves as their meeting place. What is now a flat roof will become the floor of the future worship center. About 45 people were present for the service.

After an all-too-short four days in Bucaramanga, we left for Cúcuta. The present pastor, Henoc Viera, has been a close friend to us, almost like a son. He and his wife, Ofir, have four children who call us *abuelitos* (grandparents). We joined church members on Wednesday night to help Henoc and Ofir celebrate their fourteenth wedding anniversary. Henoc and each of their children are quite talented musically, and we enjoyed hearing them play and sing. Henoc expressed interest in returning to seminary to continue his education, and we encouraged him to do so.

Time came for us to say good-bye and return to the US. We hated to leave, especially knowing that there is no Southern Baptist missionary serving in this vast area of Colombia. Is it possible that God is calling you to serve in a place like this?